OUT OF HARM'S WAY

OUT OF HARM'S WAY

Moving America's Lighthouse

Mike Booher and Lin Ezell

EASTWIND PUBLISHING
ANNAPOLIS & TRAPPE, MARYLAND USA

Published by Eastwind Publishing
Annapolis and Trappe, Maryland, U.S.A.

Eastwind Publishing
4302 Baildon Road
Trappe, MD 21673 U.S.A.
www.eastwindpublishing.com

Library of Congress Control Number 2001087242

Booher, Michael and Ezell, Lin
OUT OF HARM'S WAY
Moving America's Lighthouse

Includes bibliographical references and index

ISBN 1-885457-15-4

First Edition

Printed in Canada

For many years, Capitol Broadcasting of Raleigh, North Carolina, and its owner Jim Goodmon have generously contributed resources to projects important to the people of North Carolina.

During the Cape Hatteras Lighthouse relocation project, through their affiliate WRAL Television in Raleigh, they provided equipment and personnel to create a digital video recording of the process. This record became a part of the National Park Service archives at Cape Hatteras National Seashore. In addition, their support has made possible the production of *Out of Harm's Way*.

Capitol Broadcasting Co.

Table of Contents

*Computer visualization
of the move of the
Cape Hatteras Lighthouse
by Richard Christin*

Acknowledgements

The author and photographer wish to thank the staff of the National Park Service for access to the site and to public records and archival materials related to the Cape Hatteras Light Station. The assistance and encouragement of Bob Woody, Steve Harris, and Rob Bolling was most helpful. The entire Cape Hatteras Group made us feel like a part of the family.

Assisting with access to 19th century archival material and photographs were Sarah Downing of the Outer Banks History Center, the staff of the Old Military Branch of the National Archives and Records Administration, and the staff of the U.S. Army Military History Institute.

Rose Steinet of the National Air and Space Museum's Center for Earth and Planetary Studies helped with access to images of Earth taken by NASA astronauts from the Apollo and Shuttle programs.

Staff at International Chimney Corporation kindly reviewed the manuscript for technical accuracy. Many members of the contractor team painstakingly explained the relocation procedures during the move—to us and to countless others. Thank you for caring that we got the details right.

A special thanks goes to Helen Neuman, the author's mother, and Sally Booher, the photographer's spouse, for reviewing early drafts of the manuscript.

And, finally, a sincere debt of gratitude is due Capital Broadcasting of Raleigh, North Carolina, for their contribution in this book project. The owners and managers of Capital Broadcasting care about North Carolina history, and we hope this book helps preserve one important part of the coastal story.

Cape Hatteras
Lighthouse in 1998
before her famous
move inland.

AMERICA'S LIGHTHOUSE

Museum artifacts and historic places often evoke strong emotion. They loom larger in our minds and souls than the physical objects or structures we see before us. They become mantles for our passion, patriotism, and pride, and sometimes for our loss. These objects can be as personal as the quilt your great aunt made for her only son to set up housekeeping with; or your grandfather's pocket watch, with engraving worn faint by the press of his thumb closing it countless times; or the farm house on the prairie where your ancestors finally stopped in their trek west. Or they can be shared widely with others, the Star Spangled Banner, the Liberty Bell, the theater box in which President Lincoln was assassinated, the Wright Flyer, a tall ship under full sail, a lighthouse that stood guardian for those who needed safe passage.

Usually, it is not the museum's interpretation of these icons of American history, no matter how skilled, that makes a lasting impression on visitors. Instead, it is the physical sense of awe, the appreciation of being close to the real thing, a validation of personal feelings brought to the site. Context and condition are often more important than words of explanation. Preservation of historic places and objects so that they can be passed on to succeeding generations is paramount to the preservation of our culture. This book chronicles an unusual preservation of an icon that is both object and place. The Cape Hatteras Lighthouse of coastal North Carolina with its distinctive black and white stripes swirling around its tall tower, is instantly recognizable

Unaka Jennette, polishing the Fresnel lens of the Cape Hatteras Lighthouse. He was the last keeper of the Lighthouse Service to serve at the light. *NPS*

The lighthouse's distinctive octagonal base would be cut below ground level by an industrial saw in preparation for the long journey to its new site.

and symbolic, even to those of us who have never seen the ocean. It has become "America's Lighthouse." For residents of the Outer Banks and the millions of visitors who take refuge there, Hatteras Light reflects the traditions of another era and stands tall as a ready reminder of the solace, fury, and treachery of the sea.

Lit in 1870 to warn passing mariners of the hazards of the Diamond Shoals off Cape Hatteras, the lighthouse itself became threatened by the sea in the 20th century. The barrier island upon which it was built is slowly moving westward toward the mainland, as is the nature of such islands. And hurricanes and major storms do their part to re-shape the beaches. This shifting geography has left man-made structures on the ocean side of the island in danger of submergence. Beach-front cottages, hotels, and boardwalks have fallen victim to the sea. Portions of state route NC12 running down Hatteras Island were re-built further from the waves during the 1990s. And the Cape Hatteras Lighthouse stood within an easy stone's throw of the ocean, even though it had been constructed some 1,500 feet from the high-tide mark.

Chapter 1 of this story is the re-telling of familiar facts about the building of lighthouses at Cape Hatteras to warn mariners of the dangerous shoals that threatened coastal shipping. In Chapter 2, readers learn about efforts to stabilize the islands and preserve Hatteras Light and the beaches of the Outer Banks as part of a new national seashore. With waves nearly lapping at the base of the lighthouse, the National Park Service explored and re-explored its options in the 1970s, 1980s, and 1990s before managers made a commitment to moving it from harm's way. In Chapter 3, the reader will visit the light station and watch as the Park Service's contractors prepare to relocate the tall tower. The keepers' quarters and other ancillary structures are moved to a new site in Chapter 4. And in Chapter 5, the team pushes the lighthouse to safety as thousands watch firsthand. Television crews took the beachfront scene into homes around the world, but as intense as the coverage was, no one saw this project as keenly as the official photographer. His images bring the action and the drama of saving the lighthouse to a human scale. Chapter 6 records the reflections, lessons, and accolades of this move of the century.

International Chimney and Expert House Movers, the Park

Service's contractor team, applied the tools of the structural mover's trade to the task of moving Cape Hatteras Lighthouse, and they did so successfully. Their work was a very public demonstration of the feasibility of preserving and relocating historic structures. Should all threatened lighthouses be saved? Should all historic structures be preserved? This public project cost nearly $10 million. But even modest historic preservation projects cost dearly, whether they are the restoration of a structure or the conservation of an object. With attention to the smallest details, the need for maintaining historic integrity, the practice of using the same materials and processes as did the original builder, and the emphasis on documentation, historic preservation is labor intensive and expensive. And it is generally popular with the public and with those agencies charged with caring for the artifacts of our past.

But not every historic home, period costume, or lighthouse on the shore can be equally preserved. Degraded condition is often a limiting factor. Lack of resources is another. But even when condition, significance, technological solutions, and resources are available, the custodians of our past must set priorities and make choices.

The National Park Service wisely preserved Cape Hatteras Lighthouse, which is an icon of national significance. It was a job well done, and done under a media spotlight. But they did so not as part of a national preservation strategy. They did so at the unrelenting insistence of scientists, engineers, preservationists, and others who loved that landmark of another era. Some of those individuals badgering for action wore Park Service uniforms; many did not. Their campaign to save Hatteras Light was not carefully orchestrated, but it was a wave as large and relentless as some of the rollers brought to the shore of Hatteras Island by winter's nor'easters.

Determining what to save and how to expend our national historic preservation resources is much more difficult that figuring out how to do it. The relocation of Cape Hatteras Lighthouse, the painstaking preservation of the Star Spangled Banner, the restoration of Ellis Island, and many other notable efforts demonstrate that we can apply science, engineering, and technology to saving important relics of the past. Leading national, regional, and local agencies should now apply equal energies to developing a coordinated strategy to identify what to save from harm's way.

The masonry lighthouse tower was moved intact, including the 257 cast iron steps.

The tower of the lighthouse, originally held a first order Fresnel lens, but was replaced in 1950 after 14 years of inactivity by the automated airport type lamp shown below.

The present automated lamp in the lantern is maintained by the U.S. Coast Guard and is still part of a system warning mariners of the nearby shoals.

ABOUT THE PHOTOGRAPHY

This book highlights the photography of Mike Booher. In the 1980s, Mike and Sally Booher lived on the Outer Banks. Mike volunteered his talents as a photographer to the managers of Cape Hatteras National Seashore, capturing in his images the energy of the sea, the intensity of the visitors' experiences, and the condition of the lighthouses and other historic properties on the islands. He heard about the idea of relocating the Hatteras Lighthouse and wanted to be a part of it. But in 1991, the Boohers moved to Asheville, North Carolina, and Mike turned his attention to photography for the Park Service's Blue Ridge Parkway and other sites in the southeast. In the late 1990s, as the relocation project was finally getting under way, officials at Cape Hatteras remembered Mike's enthusiasm and skill and called on him to be the official photographer for the move in July 1998.

Mike's participation was not limited to being a man behind the lens of a camera who showed up only to record important milestones. He took up residency at the park, living in the same restored Civilian Conservation Corps cabin as had author and retired newspaper editor Ben Dixon McNeil, who wrote *The Hatteras Man* under that same roof in the 1950s. Mike was at the job site every day; he put in the same long hours as did the movers. He worked at their side, often pitching in when an extra pair of hands was needed. With hard hat, boots, and cigar, he blended in. By doing so, he gained the confidence of the participants, who grew accustomed to Mike and his camera—under the tower, on top of the tower, on scaffolding, running alongside equipment, in the cold, in the rain. As a result, he was able to document the story of the relocation in great detail and candidly. The story of the relocation wrote itself, with the help of Mike's detailed logs and images. The difficult part was selecting from the thousands of great shots.

IN MIKE'S OWN WORDS

Something historic has been accomplished. It was my good fortune to stand among giants for a short time. My life is forever altered by the experience and their friendship. In the years to come, the relocation of the Cape Hatteras Lighthouse will take its place among the historic events of the 20th century. The records will place the name of Jakubik, Matyiko, McClarren, Fischetti, Meekins, and many others alongside Simpson, Stetson and those of the 19th century who built the lighthouse. Families will seek out the names of relatives and ancestors, taking pride in their participation. On Hatteras Island, folklore and legends will take their place among the already rich heritage of the Outer Banks. My participation was a result of the efforts of Bob Woody of the National Park Service, and for this I will be forever in his debt. If I have kept a good record, it is enough. From the beginning, it was only my intent to keep a good record. I hope my children and theirs will find some pride in my contribution.

The photographic record was made using Canon cameras and lenses. The unique features and technology of the equipment made possible images I would otherwise not have gotten. The 25,000 plus images of the record were made on Fuji RAP Astia slide film, ASA 100. I wanted the images to be uniform over the 10-month period of the relocation. Every shot was a one-time opportunity.

The Slide Printer in Denver, Colorado, processed the film. They not only did their usual great processing but went the extra mile to help me keep the chronological record straight.

Thank you all. *Mike Booher*

Mike was not paid for his services. He bought his own equipment and film. The Park Service provided him the one-room cabin and complete access to the site and the project. In return, he created a complete record set of slides for the Park Service and for International Chimney, all meticulously arranged to document every detail. When there was a problem, Park Service and contractors alike called him to capture the issue photographically.

The relocation of Cape Hatteras Lighthouse was an intense life-enriching experience for the participants. But it goes beyond the intensity of the moment. This is a project that will continue to make a difference for the next 100 years for the millions who visit the coast of North Carolina and for those who care about history and the future of how we preserve our past. We are pleased to share that experience with readers of *Out of Harm's Way*.

Lin Ezell

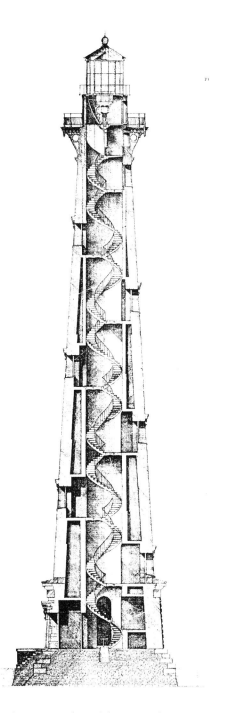

A cut-away plan of the tower shows the double wall construction and the internal structure, all of which was moved as one piece to the new location. *NPS*

CHAPTER I

LIGHTING THE SHOALS

"...many vessels are wrecked there every year; not so many now, however, as formerly, when the coast was not so well known and the lighthouses were fewer."
Captain Lyman Jackson, History of the 6th New Hampshire Regiment in the War for the Union, 1897

The American Civil War soldiers of the 6th New Hampshire Regiment knew the fury of the Atlantic Ocean off Cape Hatteras, North Carolina, firsthand. After traveling by train from New Hampshire through New York to Washington, D.C., in early January 1862, these fresh troops sailed from Annapolis, Maryland, to Fortress Monroe near Hampton, Virginia. From Hampton Roads they journeyed south to Hatteras Island aboard the side-wheel steamer *Louisiana*, en route to join General Ambrose Burnside's expedition in North Carolina. The steamer, not suited for rough sea conditions, ploughed through "one of the worst storms of that stormy coast." Two members of the regiment died before the ship finally landed on sandy beach. The soldiers, sick and cold from their near-escape from a disaster at sea, watched the debris from other ships clutter Hatteras Inlet and wash ashore. For several weeks, the regiment was encamped on Hatteras Island, "where the men suffered severely from measles, malarial fever and other diseases," with 60 deaths reported. Captain Lyman Jackson, who kept a journal during the weeks the 6th New Hampshire occupied Hatteras, made his observations of ship-wrecks and loss on the dangerous shoals off Cape Hatteras during one brief period of history.[1] In fact, these Atlantic waters are the gravesite for

H. Bamber, engineer for the Lighthouse Board, took this photograph of the lighthouse at Cape Hatteras in 1893. *National Archives.*

1

The 1938 remains of the G. A. Kohler, a steam schooner out of Baltimore, can still be seen on the shore at Hatteras Island

Photographed by the crew of Apollo 9 in March 1969, the North Carolina Outer Banks are the eastern-most landform of the southern United States. Cape Lookout can be located near the bottom of the image; Cape Hatteras, in the center, juts out into the Atlantic. The large inland bodies of water are the Pamlico and Albemarle Sounds.
National Aeronautics and Space Administration

hundreds of eighteenth, nine-teenth, and twentieth century vessels that were attempting the run up or down the American East Coast.

Hatteras Island is one of a chain of barrier islands, known as the Outer Banks, which buffers the mainland of North Carolina from the force of the ocean. Part of the Carolinas island chain extends some 40 miles off the mainland. The lower Outer Banks landform, which includes Hatteras, stretches among four major capes and is the easternmost point of the southern United States. The islands are 3.5 miles at their widest point but narrow to less than 600 feet.

Being on these off-shore islands is much like being at sea. The wind blows constantly. Seasonal temperature ranges are narrower. Powerful storms lash the islands with fury.

Sea conditions near the Outer Banks are often treacherous: two strong ocean currents collide there—the southward-flowing Virginia Drift, the southern most tip of the Arctic Labrador Current, *and* the warm waters of the north-bound Gulf Stream. This junction of currents is also the site of three sandy, shallow, ever-shifting shoals. Once known as the Cape Hatteras Shoals, the trio was officially designated Diamond Shoals by the U.S. Board of Geographic Names in 1949, named after the shape of the inner-most shoal. Hatteras Island makes an abrupt turn from its north-south orientation to an east-west run, but sand, pushed by the along-shore currents, continues to drift in a southerly direction out to sea at the elbow of this turn. Although European mariners exploring the New World had never heard of the term "littoral drift," they knew of the 14-mile stretch of shallow shoals.

Captains of the Colonial period through the nineteenth century respected or feared those waters as they transported goods and passengers between northern and southern ports, but they did not avoid them. Ships heading north could save many days by riding the currents of the Gulf Stream and catching prevailing southwest winds. Vessels bound the other direction would ride the Virginia Drift, but at the junction of the two currents the captains needed the right wind conditions to negotiate safely the passage between the shoals and the Gulf Stream. Before ships could round Cape Hatteras, they often had to wait several days for winds that would assure them safe passage. Frequently, the wait brought storms instead. Blind in a raging storm with no open seas in which to ride out the conditions, sails were torn from their riggings, masts splintered, and ships floundered on the shoals with little chance for recovery.

Would a beacon visible from Diamond Shoals marking the point of Cape Hatteras help the captains?

As early as 1715, merchants in the colony of Massachusetts, frustrated by maritime losses, had funded the construction of a lighthouse to mark the Boston harbor. Because commercial losses from shipwrecks were a major concern to the young government— and because maritime commerce was booming in the years that followed the war with England —President George Washington chose Alexander Hamilton, Secretary of the Treasury, to solve the problem in North Carolina. Washington made a good choice in Hamilton, who, as a young man, had experienced the power and terror of the seas near the Diamond Shoals onboard the *Thunderbolt.* On a north-bound journey to Boston, Hamilton's ship had become disabled and narrowly escaped the treacherous waters that had claimed so many vessels.

Through the Lighthouse Bill of 1789, Congress authorized Hamilton to oversee aids to navigation, including lighthouse maintenance and construction, in an attempt to make commerce along the coast safer and more profitable. Within Treasury, the U.S. Lighthouse Establishment would oversee this important work. The new bill relieved the individual states of the expense and responsibility of building and maintaining lighthouses. Hamilton soon directed

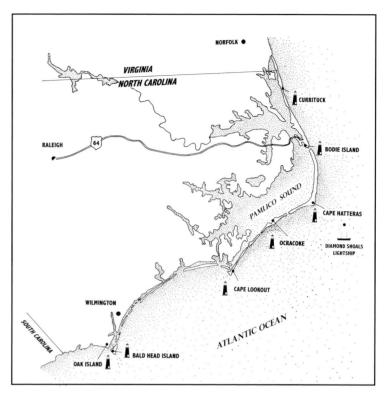

North Carolina's coastal lighthouses. *Drawing by Vincent Wright*

The Dearborn tower as depicted in 1870 by George B. Nicholson, 5th District Assistant Engineer. It shows the original tower and the 1854 addition.

U.S. Coast Guard

his Commissioner of Revenue, Tenche Cox, to explore the feasibility of building a lighthouse on Cape Hatteras that would warn vessels of the dangerous shoals so close to the shipping lanes.

Lighthouses serve as aides to maritime navigation, usually as tower-like structures located in coastal areas or anchored in the seabed off-shore. In 280 B.C., Egyptians built a 350-foot lighthouse in the harbor of Alexandria, and the Phoenicians and Romans relied on lighthouses during the early centuries A.D. Lighthouse design as we know it today dates from the eighteenth century. Towers were constructed first from wood, then masonry; modern structures are made from concrete and steel. A lighthouse can be identified by its distinctive shape and color as a daymarker and by the flash pattern of its light. By the eighteenth century, wood, coal, and candles as sources of illumination for lighthouses had given way to oil lamps, which were replaced by electricity in the twentieth century. Rotating mirrors and then lenses were used to intensify the beacons. Modern lighthouses can be equipped with audible warning devices, radio and radar beacons, and computerized weather stations. Although increasingly sophisticated satellite-based navigation systems have decreased the necessity for tall lighthouses that mark the land and warn mariners of danger, smaller structures are still used to navigate in crowded coastal areas and shipping lanes.

In 1794, Congress approved the building of a lighthouse at Cape Hatteras and another on a sand mound called Bald Head on Smith Island to guide vessels to the mouth of the Cape Fear River, some 170 miles south of the proposed Hatteras beacon. The Bald Head project already had been approved by the North Carolina General Assembly in 1784 and was likely under construction but not complete at the time of federal approval in 1789. A third lighthouse for the region, on Ocracoke Island, also had been approved previously by the state in 1789. The Governor of North Carolina deeded land for the Bald Head and Ocracoke lighthouses to the Federal government in 1790. Two years later, Congress approved funding for completion of Bald Head Light, North Carolina's first lighthouse. It became operational in 1795. Closer to Hatteras, entrepreneurs had built a shipping center on a massive oyster bed called Old Rock, later named Shell Castle Island, near Ocracoke Inlet. In 1794, Congress authorized construction of a 55-foot wooden light to guide the many shipping vessels bound for this increasingly busy port.

After three years of delays in securing land for a lighthouse on Hatteras, in 1797 Commissioner Cox purchased a four-acre tract on the eastern-most pitch of the island from the Jennett family for $50. Cox's search for a reliable builder for the new aid required several advertisements nation-wide, and he rejected the first round of bids. Major Henry Dearborn, Congressman from Massachusetts, submitted a satisfactory bid to construct both the Hatteras and Shell Castle structures. His proposal was one of three forwarded to President John Adams. However, before the President could complete his review, William Miller, Jr., replaced Cox as Commissioner of Revenue. Asking for more details in the cost proposals, Miller pulled all the bids and invited the builders to resubmit. In the fall of 1798, Miller accepted Dearborn's bid for the construction of both lighthouses for $38,450, and Congress released the first $8,000 to purchase building materials for Hatteras.

Cape Lookout Lighthouse was the first of the new North Carolina coastal towers built in 1859. *Mariners' Museum*

It was late summer 1799 before Dearborn, his crew, and the first load of materials arrived on Hatteras Island, having sailed up the Pamlico Sound and docked on the sound side of the island more than a mile from the construction site. Materials had to be transported across sand and marsh by oxen team. Needing immediate accommodations for his workforce, Dearborn first built the quarters that would subsequently be provided for the two keepers of the lighthouse once it was operational, a two-story wooden structure, originally 34 feet by 16 feet. In December, he declared an end to the first construction season and dismissed his crew.

The second year saw the completion of the foundation and construction of part of the Hatteras tower before the workers' health problems dragged the project to a standstill. During the 1801 season, the men fared no better, and the tower was again left uncompleted. With each summer came debilitating sickness on an island the workers shared with swarms of disease-carrying mosquitoes. The octagonal brown Hatteras Lighthouse was not placed in operation until the fall of 1803, 14 years after Hamilton asked if such a light was feasible. Atop a 90-foot tower made of granite and sandstone, the lantern room sent a signal to sea designed to warn mariners of the Diamond Shoals, 15 miles off the beach.

The Hatteras beacon failed. It was not bright enough to mark

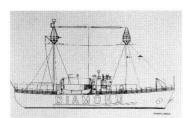

LIGHTSHIPS

Lightships are vessels specially rigged with beacons on their masts and anchored at sea near some land feature, mark, or hazard to serve as a warning light for vessels under way. Each ship was numbered and its station name painted on both sides of the ship for easy identification. The first American lightship was assigned to mark Willoughby Spit near Norfolk, Virginia, in 1820. Congress authorized funding in 1823 for a second much larger light vessel to serve on the Diamond Shoals. From 1825 to 1836, nine other lit anchored vessels, with their twin lights fixed 40 feet above the water, were sent to duty stations along the North Carolina coast to mark sounds, shoals, and river channels between the Outer Banks and the mainland. Duty aboard a lightship was hazardous, monotonous, and seemingly never-ending, but the lightships provided warning beacons where lighthouses were not practical, or they supplemented beacons that could not reach far enough to provide mariners with an acceptable margin of safety. They could pull anchor and position themselves elsewhere as needed, and they could serve as sound signal stations in times of reduced visibility or be outfitted as transmitters of electronic signals for bearings and distance finding. The last lightship off the North Carolina coast pulled up her anchor for the final time in 1967.

the shoals, and captains, ship owners, and merchants complained that often the light was extinguished when they needed its guidance most. To address the lighthouse's shortcomings, officials of the U.S. Lighthouse Establishment doubled the capacity of the oil storage cisterns and installed a wire enclosure around the exterior of the lantern room to prevent birds from flying into and cracking the windows. But the lamps themselves were the problem.

The Hatteras Lighthouse's lamps produced high heat in the small, contained space of the lantern room. Fires were not uncommon. In 1812, the lantern system was replaced with new lamps and parabolic reflectors patented by Winslow Lewis. Higher quality oil was provided for the lamps in 1817, and the Government hired a new keeper in the hope of bringing improved operations to the tower. Dissatisfaction, however, continued, prompting the Government to place an anchored "lightship" at the outer edge of the Diamond Shoals, 15 miles off Hatteras Island, to supplement Hatteras Light in 1824. The large ship, built by Henry Eckford of New York, bore the name *Cape Hatteras* and was equipped with two lanterns fixed aloft on masts. She was blown ashore and wrecked near Ocracoke Inlet during a storm three years later.

A second problem plagued the lighthouse on Hatteras. The foundation, which had been set 13 feet below the surface, was being exposed by constant winds. As early as 1810, sand had eroded from the base, exposing four feet of foundation. Over the next 40 years, erosion continued, and in 1850 a fence was built at the lighthouse's base to save it.

Hatteras' lamps were outfitted with new reflectors in 1835 and 1845. A completely new lantern system was installed in 1848. But it was not until 1854 that the long-demanded improvements were made. Reacting to criticism leveled by a panel of experts that had been asked by Congress to investigate the American lighthouse system, the lawmakers approved sweeping changes for the light. The Lighthouse Review Board, in its 700-page report, had judged Hatteras Light to be in the most need of renovations of any light on the coast. In 1854, the height was increased to 150 feet, a first-order Fresnel lens system was installed, and the tower was painted to improve its day-time visibility (red over white). Finally, ships could see the warning light and hope to avoid the Diamond Shoals.

Engineer and physicist Augustin-Jean Fresnel (1788-1827) of France developed the use of compound lenses instead of mirrors

The Three Lighthouses at Cape Hatteras

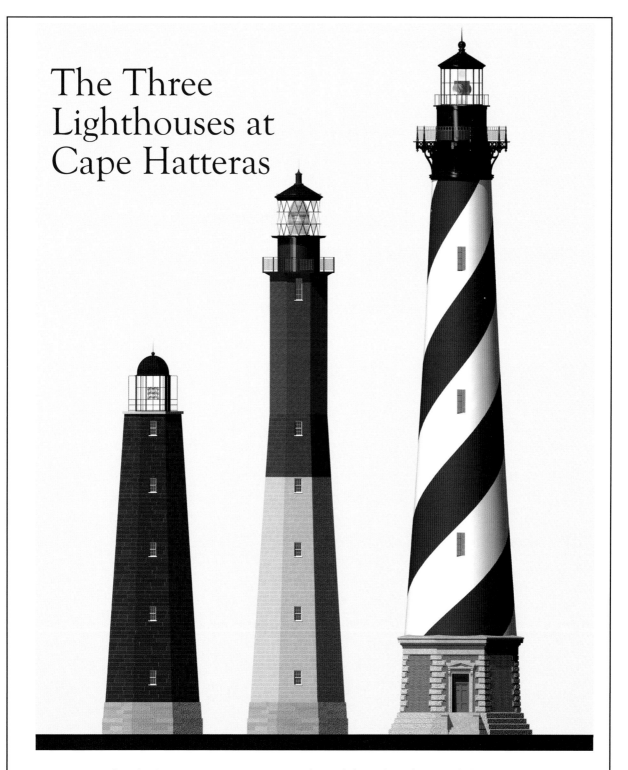

Henry Dearborn's 1803 Hatteras Lighthouse, constructed of granite and brown sandstone, proved a poor day marker, since it did not contrast with the sandy beach upon which it was built.

To improve the visibility of the original Hatteras tower, it was painted red over white in 1854 and increased in height to150'.

The 1870 lighthouse was originally painted red over white. The distinctive black and white stripes were ordered in 1873.

Computer visualization by Richard Christin

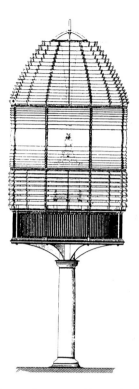

A first order Fresnel lens, the largest ever used, was originally installed in the lantern at Cape Hatteras. The lamp was rotated by a clockwork mechanism powered by descending weights. The Cape Hatteras Fresnel lens was both a fixed and a flashing light in which the mariner would see a steady light, interrupted by a flashing light.
Courtesy Eastwind Publishing

for lighthouses. He surrounded a lamp with a ring of optic glass, with the prisms angled so as to concentrate 90 percent of the lamp's light and magnify its power. His lens and the single-wick lamp replaced the multiple reflectors previously used in lighthouses.

There were six classes of Fresnel lenses, based on size, and four other modifications that were manufactured in smaller numbers. The first-order lens was the largest, 10 feet tall, with a 36.2-inch radius. A sixth-order lens, 18 inches in height, had a radius of 5.9 inches. The Lighthouse Board installed a first-order Fresnel lens in the lantern room of Hatteras Light in 1854, improving its visibility by ships in the vicinity of the Diamond Shoals.

During the first year of the American Civil War (1861-1865), Confederate soldiers controlled the strategic navigational aids off coastal North Carolina and darkened the lighthouses that might have guided Union warships or aided commercial vessels supporting the North. Soldiers wearing gray removed Cape Hatteras' Fresnel lens to the mainland, and Confederates used the tower as a lookout for sea-going targets against which Southern privateers could prey. In August 1861, Union troops took Hatteras Island and successfully defended the lighthouse from a planned Southern assault that fall. The men of the Third Georgia had fully intended to destroy the lighthouse on Hatteras. Responding to many calls from Northern mariners to re-light Hatteras, the Lighthouse Board, as the Lighthouse Establishment had been known since 1852, installed a more readily available but less powerful second-order Fresnel lens in 1862. The following year, Hatteras Light was again equipped with a first-order lens. The Board's chief engineer, however, noted that the structure itself was in degraded condition, having suffered from the brutal environment of sand, sea, and air.

Dearborn's lighthouse on Hatteras had an unstable foundation, expanding cracks, aging wooden stairs, and degraded iron work. The cost of repairs would exceed the cost of a new lighthouse, reported the Lighthouse Board's district engineer. A new lighthouse at Hatteras would also fit the Board's master plan for a series of additional coastal towers approximately 40 miles apart from Cape Henry in southern Virginia to Cape Hatteras. Ships were still being lost along this stretch of coast, and the Board was anxious to fill the void in the coastal navigation scheme. Vessels making their way along the coast in sight of these lights would be able to pick up the beacon ahead before losing the one just passed.

The plan demanded tall lighthouses equipped with powerful beacons. The model for new lighthouses at Hatteras, Bodie Island, and Currituck Beach was Cape Lookout Light, completed in 1859. It was designed "in house" by the engineering talent of the Lighthouse Board.

Congress appropriated $75,000 for a new lighthouse at Cape Hatteras in 1867 and added another $40,000 shortly thereafter when the Lighthouse Board determined that the new beacon should shine from a height of 180 feet instead of 150 feet. The Board, adamant that this new first-order tower be made of the best materials and that its construction be of the highest caliber, took on the construction job itself. Dexter Stetson of Maine, an accomplished builder with lighthouse construction experience, was hired by Lighthouse Board District Engineer W. J. Newman to supervise the project in late 1868. Location of the new structure was also a concern. In its 1869 annual report, the Board pointed out that the site of the new lighthouse would be "above the highest level of the sea and so far removed from the waterline as to render it safe from encroachment from the sea."

The Board designed the lighthouse built at Cape Hatteras, and Brevet Brigadier General James Hervey Simpson and his assistant engineers oversaw Stetson's construction of it. Simpson inspected and approved work in progress, verified that the design was being faithfully executed, and took delivery of the finished product.

The Lighthouse Board let contracts for more than one million red bricks for the tower, Vermont stone for the foundation and steps, oil tanks, and metal work, as well as for transportation of all these materials to Hatteras Island. Stetson, arriving on site in late 1868, first built quarters for his work crew, a blacksmith shop, storage buildings, and lifting derricks, just as Major Dearborn had done many years before. But Stetson also built three scows, smaller work boats, to shuttle building materials from delivery vessels anchored in Pamlico Sound to a new long wharf constructed by the lighthouse crew. A tram railway was Stetson's final supply link to the construction site.

Supplies and materials were late in arriving to the lighthouse construction crew. One shipment of granite was lost on its way to the wharf, and two loads of bricks, along with the ships carrying them, sank in storms. In early 1869, 600 feet northeast of

Gen James Hervey Simpson

Shortly after Lighthouse Board Engineer W. J. Newman hired a crew to build the new Lighthouse at Hatteras in late 1868, Brevet Brigadier General James Hervey Simpson (1813-1883) took his place as chief engineer of the Fifth Lighthouse District, which included North Carolina. In the late 1840s, Simpson, with the U.S. Army Corps of Topographical Engineers, had been charged with harbor improvements on Lake Erie and oversaw the construction of West Sister Island Lighthouse in Michigan's Maumee Bay in 1848. This light was one of six built by the Corps of Topographical Engineers for the Lighthouse Establishment during this period. In the years before the Civil War, Simpson, a West Point graduate, explored the southwest, mapping new overland mail routes, surveying remote deserts and mountains, and collecting information about Native American cultures and languages. During the last year of the War, the Army promoted him to Brevet Brigadier General in recognition of his service, especially to General Burnside for whom he had overseen the building of "strong and defensive works along so great a portion of our lines."

U.S. Army Military History Institute

FIRST ORDER
LIGHT HOUSE
for
CAPE HATTERAS, N.C.
1869

After Cape Hatteras Lighthouse was built, Captain Peter C. Harris, engineer, transmitted these marked plans to the Lighthouse Board in April 1871. In ink, Harris noted the weight of all the building components on this set of plans. *National Archives*

Dearborn's tower, Stetson commenced work, with the excavation of a hole six feet deep. Unable to drive pilings into the hard compacted sand to support the massive lighthouse's foundation as called for in the specifications, Stetson pumped the fresh water from the hole he had dug and laid layers of yellow pine timbers in the bottom. Granite rubble atop the pine served as the base for stone footers, and when the stone reached a level above the water table, the crew re-flooded the excavation. The submerged pine timbers would not decay and would provide a suitable foundation for the octagonal cut granite and brick base, which was completed by the end of the year. But problems with transporting construction materials to the remote site and illness among the workers prevented the foreman from starting work on the brick tower on schedule.

In 1870, Stetson augmented his workforce with laborers from the island, and his masons worked steadily on the pair of concentric brick walls that formed the tower. They built nine landings, each with a window, as they worked their way to the top, where customized iron work for the lantern room embellished the structure. In December, the lampist installed the lens, tested the machinery, and lit the new 208-foot-tall Hatteras Light. The tallest lighthouse in the country began warning ships off the Diamond Shoals.

Plans called for the second Hatteras Lighthouse to bear the same color scheme as the first. Accordingly, Stetson's crew whitewashed the interior and painted the exterior red over white. Cape Hatteras Light's distinctive black and white stripes would not be ordered

until 1873. An iron fence to discourage grazing livestock completed the lighthouse grounds. The lighthouse construction crew had already renovated the existing keepers' quarters and used excess bricks from the lighthouse job site to build a smaller dwelling for the principal keeper and his family. Three keepers, instead of two, would be required on station to maintain the new beacon. Stetson moved north to Bodie Island in June 1871 to start the process all over again. In late 1870, with the new lighthouse station nearly complete, Simpson was re-assigned to the Eighth Lighthouse District headquarters in Mobile, Alabama.

The keepers of the lighthouse lived close by. The principal keeper and his family occupied a two-story brick home, while the two assistant keepers lived in a wooden dwelling large enough for their wives and children. Note the flooding behind the keepers' quarters in this 1893 photograph by Engineer Bamber. *National Archives*

CHAPTER II

THE SEA COMES TO CAPE HATTERAS

"Ringing almost every gently sloping coast in the world are narrow strips of sand called barrier islands. These fascinating islands, capable of actually migrating landward when the sea level rises, are both the most dynamic and the most sought-after real estate in the world." —*Orrin H. Pilkey et al., The North Carolina Shore and Its Barrier Islands.*

In 1870, the new Cape Hatteras Lighthouse sent its much-needed warning signal to the vicinity of the Diamond Shoals, where as many as 50 ships a day were navigating the merging currents. Remains of the first tower were destroyed in 1871. The following year, Dexter Stetson completed Hatteras' sister light at Bodie Island, approximately 40 miles to the north. But even the brightest lights from shore could not always protect ships from being savaged by the fierce storms that visited those waters. Losses continued, as did complaints about those losses. A light on the shoals themselves might help keep ships clear of the area, giving captains a warning on the horizon as they approached the danger zone. Hatteras Light, 19 miles away, could be seen under optimum conditions from the outer shoals, but that could be too late. When hurricane winds threatened the loaded schooners, they needed plenty of deep water in which to ride out the storm. If they were already too close to the Diamond Shoals when fierce storms struck them, their chances of survival were greatly diminished.

Responding to the losses at sea, in 1884 the Lighthouse Board placed a whistling buoy on the Shoals, but it fared no better than other early attempts at anchoring marker buoys or a lightship on those shifting sandy shoals. Late in the decade, the U.S. Army Corps of Engineers gave thought to the design of an offshore tower anchored with a steel or cast iron caisson sunk into the sea floor.

As late as the 1930s ships were washed ashore on the Outer Banks. This schooner wrecked, along with its cargo of lumber, off Ocracoke Island in 1936. *NPS*

Light Vessel 69 took her post at the Diamond Shoals in 1897. With two beacons, the lightship helped warn mariners of the dangerous shoals, supplementing Cape Hatteras Light. The Diamond lightships also carried steam chime whistles to signal their position during fog. Number 69 is shown here after being blown onshore after a hurricane in 1899.
P. Hornberger Collection

In 1890, bids were opened for the off-shore tower project, estimated to cost in the range of $300,000 to $500,000. Construction began the next year. But currents pulled hard at the footholds of the caisson, and a storm washed away the efforts to construct the foundation. Rather than start again, the monies left from the Congressional appropriation went toward funding a new Diamond Shoals lightship, designated Light Vessel (LV) 69 by the Light house Board.

Bath Iron Works of Maine built the vessel, which was over 122 feet long, powered by steam, with a steel frame and wooden hull. With her two beacons, she arrived on station approximately 15 miles from the lighthouse in September 1897. LV69 recorded the passing of 3,878 ships during her first six months at anchor. While the Lighthouse Board considered two other designs for off-shore towers in the last years of the 19th century and early in the 20th, the organization put its faith instead in light vessels and ever-improving mooring anchors and chains. Light Vessel 71, a sister ship from Bath Iron Works, supplemented and then replaced Vessel 69 when she was assigned elsewhere in 1901, and LV 72 joined watch duty in the early years of the new century. A product of Fore River Shipbuilding Company of Massachusetts, Vessel 72 was a steel-hull ship over 123 feet long, powered by steam. From 1823 to 1966, six lightships served at the Cape Hatteras Station. The first ship was named *Cape Hatteras* while the latter ships all bore the name *Diamond* or *Diamond Shoal* or *Diamond Shoals.* [1]

Improvements to Cape Hatteras Light's lamp and the effectiveness of the lightships meant fewer losses of cargo and life. And ships were stronger and mechanically powered, no longer dependent only on favorable winds and currents. During the years leading to America's late involvement in the First World War, life at Hatteras Light Station took on a rhythm of important routine, still isolated from the villages but closer each year to the waves of the Atlantic.

German submarines became the principal threat to ships off the North Carolina Coast during World War I, not the Diamond Shoals. It was estimated that 100 ships were destroyed by lurking U-boats in the vicinity of the Outer Banks where they were unprotected and vulnerable. The crew of Light Vessel 71 saw this action in close quarters in August 1918. After witnessing the sinking of a passing freighter, they radioed a warning to coastal traffic. For their efforts, U-boat 104 sunk the unarmed and anchored LV 71 with surface gunfire, but after its crew was advised of the pending action by the sub's captain and took to life boats. In 1922, Vessel 105 (later designated WAL 527) took her turn on Diamond Shoals. Built by Consolidated Shipbuilding Company of New York, she was more than 146 feet long, with a steel hull and two masts. Her equipment included a radio and radio beacon.

In this 1985 work, maritime artist Tom Freeman captures Light Vessel 71 as it is being attacked by a German submarine during World War I off Cape Hatteras. The painting hangs in Park Service offices at Manteo, North Carolina. *Courtesy of the artist and the National Park Service.*

S haped by the relentless waves and visited by frequent storms, the flat sandy ocean-side coastline of Hatteras Island was always on the move. During some years, the breakers were closer to the lighthouse than others, but the slope of the beach increased as land submerged. The new tower had been built safely more than 1,500 feet from the high-tide mark of 1870, and assumedly the authorities did not worry about its proximity to the ocean, but each year brought the waters 25 feet closer to the light. In 1919, the ocean was less than 300 feet away, and that did not escape the attention of residents and officials of the Bureau of Lighthouses, the latest title for the service charged with caring for aids to navigation.

Freely grazing livestock on Hatteras Island had eaten the grasses and shrubs that once grew from the sandy soil. In 1919, vegetation was replanted, and dune construction began along the shore of this island, which was still sparsely populated by fishermen and isolated from the mainland.[2] But by the 1930s, this isolation started to dissolve. Bridges spanned the Roanoke and Currituck Sounds to the north, and the sand tracks that had serviced vehicular traffic on the northern Outer Banks were replaced with paved roads. Visitors and residents alike, however, still depended on ferries to cross Oregon and Hatteras Inlets, and this inconvenience delayed

Number 71 and number 69 both served at the Diamond Shoal station between 1898 and 1900. Number 71 went on to serve alternately at the station for another 18 years before being sunk by the U-boat.
P. Hornberger Collection

16

A Civilian Conservation Corps camp was built just off the beach near Cape Hatteras Lighthouse. Thousands of men were "enrolled" in the Corps and sent to work camps across the country, many of which were managed by the National Park Service. Camps on the Outer Banks provided manpower for stabilizing the beaches. *North Carolina Deparment of Conservation and Development, 1936*

development of the southern Banks.

In the 1930s, land submergence— identified and treated as beach erosion— again caught the attention of Hatteras Lighthouse watchers. Experts continued to advise that grasses and trees would stabilize the beach. And wind fences would capture sand and build dunes, which would serve as a defense line against the sea washing overland. But this time, local residents were assisted in their efforts by the Civilian Conservation Corps (CCC).

As part of the national effort to employ large numbers of Americans thrown out of work during the Depression, the CCC established camps across the country from which major public works projects were accomplished, including beach stabilization on Hatteras. Nearly 500 Civilian Conservation Corps companies with 100,000 enrollees operated under the technical supervision of the Park Service by the mid-1930s, with nearly 100 units in parks and at monuments. The National Park Service, recognizing the future potential for the establishment of a national recreational area along the Outer Banks, took over the management of the CCC camps at Cape Hatteras in an attempt to stop beach erosion there. The Corps planted sea oats, grasses, shrubs, and trees by the thousands and strung miles of brush, wire, and slat fences. Others tried pumping sand, replenishing it where it was "needed." Their work was not guided by a scientific understanding of the dynamics of barrier islands and their natural move westward toward the mainland. Stabilizing the beaches against future losses made sense at the time.

When major hurricanes lashed out at the islands in 1933, the government significantly increased its support to stabilize the beaches. At the lighthouse, storm waters from the second storm of that year gutted the two keepers' quarters and water crept up the long flight of stairs in the tower, which swayed with the hurricane's force. The three keepers kept their vigil in the lighthouse and kept the light aflame through the long night. By 1934, however, they no longer worried about keeping the oil-burning mantle lamp replenished during terrible storms. Electric generators and batteries were installed in the oil house and an electric bulb in the lantern room.

Miles of fences were built to capture sand and build dunes. Fence designs that relied on driftwood prompted crews to gather deadwood and cut brush.
North Carolina Department of Conservation and Development, 1936

Alocal constituency of property owners became interested in preserving the southern Outer Banks as public park land in 1933. When National Park Service Associate Director A. E. Demaray told them in late 1934 that the Service was "favorably impressed" with the potential of the North Carolina coast, the owners pledged the donation of 1,000 acres and 55 miles of coast. Although Park Service Director Arno B. Cammerer was originally not convinced that Cape Hatteras was a viable candidate for a park "under existing standards as a member of the national park system," Demaray countered in a handwritten note that it was "probably the outstanding example of a type of characteristic scenery not now preserved. . . . I would say it met the standards prescribed for national parks."[3]   North Carolina, believing in the urgency to stabilize the islands for the benefit of public and private uses, joined the efforts to save them, but as a 1,400-acre state park, which could be transferred to the Federal government as a national park at a later date. Henry Phipps, a businessman from New York who frequented Hatteras to hunt and fish, donated nearly 1,000 of those acres to North Carolina, just south of Cape Hatteras Lighthouse at Cape Point.

A small number of local land owners who favored the Park Service's intervention on the Outer Banks wrote numerous letters to Washington officials during the 1930s, attempting to facilitate and broker the acquisition of lands for the park unit. Letterheads included: Atlantic Coast Sportsmen's Association, North Carolina Coastal Commission, and Dare County Development Company. During 1934 and 1935, the Park Service wished to keep its preliminary investigations of the Outer Banks relatively quiet, but one supporter provided information to the local press in August 1935, which evoked a handwritten note from George M. Wright, Chief of the Park Service's Wildlife Division: "I favor a sound spanking" for the author of the news leak.[4] From past experiences, the Park Service knew that land values could escalate considerably once speculators knew of the agency's interests in an area. While the Park Service's "friends" insisted that their interests in the project

CCC workers harvested grasses in nurseries on-site and planted the vegetation along the beach. *North Carolina Department of Conservation and Development, 1936*

were philanthropic, the agency used caution in its relationship with the Outer Banks property owners.

While the Park Service was investigating the feasibility of creating this new park unit in North Carolina, the sea reached the base of Hatteras Light in 1936, despite attempts at protection by so many. The structure itself was in good condition when the keepers were forced to turn off the light and lock the doors on May 15th. In 1939, the U.S. Coast Guard assumed responsibility for all lighthouse operations in the country, taking over the work of the dissolved Bureau of Lighthouses. But at Hatteras that amounted to watching over a 150-foot skeleton steel tower with a substitute light, in-shore near Buxton Woods, 1,800 yards from the Lighthouse. The "temporary" tower had been erected in 1935 at a cost of $5,868 and lit the following year.

Shortly after the keepers left Hatteras Lighthouse to the waves, the Park Service inquired about using some of the ancillary station buildings to support their work with the CCC. In July 1936, the agency asked the Department of Commerce, to whom the Bureau of Lighthouses reported, about the probability of securing the defunct lighthouse itself to "preserve it as part of the general development of the North Carolina sea coast...." The Bureau of Lighthouses had declared the entire 44-acre complex surplus to its needs.[5]

A Park Service historian noted in 1936 that the Hatteras Lighthouse would give the agency "an opportunity to present an instructive picture of nineteenth century American shipping." This historical site would complement the large recreational acreage the Park Service was considering for its first national seashore. When North Carolina Congressman Lindsay C. Warren learned of the Park Service's interest, he wrote to Interior Secretary Harold L. Ickes that the Service should acquire the entire barrier island zone from Oregon Inlet to Cape Lookout: 36,000 acres, which could be purchased for $710,000. [6]

Officials at the Park Service envisioned a seashore that would be preserved in its natural state and protected from aggressive commercial seaside development. They would discourage further highway construction and oppose a bridge over Oregon Inlet. This point of view contrasted sharply with an editorial from a local Outer Banks newspaper. Upon hearing the news that the Park Service was interested in establishing a large park in the area, the author wrote that Dare County was headed for a gigantic future of progress and development.

> As one begins to think of the hundreds of thousands of
> dollars that are to be spent, of the hundreds of men who
> will be on the Federal payrolls drawing money to turn
> loose, of the tremendous increase in activity, travel and
> business that will result from these Government enter-
> prises, it is staggering to the imagination to consider that
> this will put more prosperity in Dare County by many
> times over than has ever been known here before.[7]

The Director's personal assistant did not favor establishing a "park" on the Outer Banks, because, he said, parks are preserved, not built. He wrote that a Cape Hatteras park would have to be "built—the soil, the vegetative cover, the roads and accommodations—from almost a Palaeozoic nothingness." Instead he urged the Park Service to write its own prescription for national beaches, which should be "unspoiled, extensive, and suitable for a national playground."[8] In 1936, Congress passed the Park, Parkway and Recreation-Area Act, which reinforced the Park Service's call for a comprehensive study of these new categories of lands that would be overseen by the agency.[9]

In August 1936, the Acting Treasury Secretary approved the transfer of "Cape Hatteras Lighthouse Station Reservation" to the Park Service, which promised to maintain it as a "valuable relic of America's maritime history." But the Fresnel lens was not part of the transfer because it was still serviceable and could be needed elsewhere in the lighthouse network. The Federal lighthouse managers allowed the Park Service to keep the lens in place, however, and include it as a visitor attraction. After taking physical delivery of the lighthouse in November, E. J. Byrum, the Park Service's newly appointed project superintendent at Hatteras, presented Washington with his first proposal for repairs: just a small amount of work was needed to keep the rain out, at a cost of $200.[10]

When Byrum first arrived, the beach nearest the Light Station was still a "flat, sandy waste, void of vegetation, and inundated by

Frank Stick, a local land owner who enthusiastically identified lands for donation and purchase for the new park unit, often served as escort and local guide during visits by Park Service officials. Shown here during such a trip in 1934, catching channel bass, from left to right, are Harry C. Lawrence and Hugh A. Campbell, colleagues of Stick's, Stick, and Horace Dough, Park Service custodian at Kill Devil Hill Monument, a memorial to the Wright brothers' first powered flight. *NPS, 1934*

water at every extremely high tide." And the CCC's camp surgeon had set up shop in the larger keepers' quarters. He soon was busy building sand fences and planning structural improvements to all the buildings at the station. Byrum was especially successful at enlisting the help of the Conservation Corps in preserving the lighthouse grounds, outbuildings, and the tower itself. He fretted that when CCC Camp NP-1 at Buxton was disbanded in 1940 that "it will be necessary to provide protection for the property or practically lose what has already been done in the way of restoring and equipping the lighthouse buildings."[11]

Park Service officials continued to concur that Cape Hatteras should not be given the status of a park, as traditionally defined. In their recommendations to Acting Secretary of Interior Charles West, they observed:

> . . . since the ocean beaches constitute a limited and
> rapidly diminishing national resource, large sections of
> which should be preserved for the public benefit and use,
> it is recommended that a suitable portion of this area be
> acquired by the Federal Government and be designated as
> a National Seashore.

West sent Congressman Warren draft language for legislation in May 1937, and Congress passed the bill to establish Cape Hatteras National Seashore in August. There would be no land purchases for the new unit, however. The House Committee on Public Lands stipulated that no public funds were to be used to secure property. Only public or private donations could be relied upon to build the seashore.[12] To facilitate these donations, the General Assembly of North Carolina created an 11-member Seashore Commission.

While waiting for the lands to be donated, Park Service officials began to define the new unit's property boundaries and create a master plan. They renovated the lighthouse station's keepers' quarters, which were being used as the Cape Hatteras Lighthouse Lodge managed by a concessionaire, and painted the 208-foot-high tower. One planner predicted that visitors would be unable to resist stopping at this new tourist destination and climbing its 257 steps. But because those new tourists would be traveling to Cape Hatteras in primitive conditions, it might also be necessary "to provide motor repair facilities along the way since the existing sand road causes unusual wear on automotive equipment necessitating frequent repairs." They worried that novice drivers would become stranded. "In lieu of an improved highway, it may be necessary to have one or two automobile relief stations," the Plans and Design Branch wrote. And cabins, hotels, and campgrounds would be needed.[13]

During the 1930s, officials from the National Park Service trekked to the Outer Banks on fact-finding missions. Their first obstacle was crossing Oregon Inlet by ferry. *NPS, 1934*

Other members of the Cape Hatteras development team turned their attention to natural resource needs. In a memo that reflected thinking ahead of the times, one manager passed on the findings of a staff biologist. In performing their work, CCC enrollees had disturbed the habitat of the Island, the report said. Marshes had been altered; deadwood removed; fresh water holes drained; roadways built over breeding grounds for shore birds. Besides acquiring land for a wide range of recreational uses, the Park Service must also consider the special needs of historical, geological, and wildlife interests. Another prescient minority voice came from the Park Service's Naturalist Division. The coastline is sinking very slowly, Earl A. Trager said. Unless we can "control the power of the waves and the force of the wind the bar will surely . . . march westward." He warned his colleagues to use caution as they considered plans for re-forestation and dune construction on Hatteras Island.[14] In 1940, Congress amended the enabling legislation, changing the designation of the unit to Cape Hatteras National Seashore Recreational Area. But war in Europe and then in the Pacific diverted resources and attention to matters of more critical national importance than preserving beaches and historic structures.

The 19th century brick tower was pressed into service again, this time as a lookout for Coast Guardsmen scouting for German submarines known to frequent the American east coast. The seas over which the Hatteras Light had shown came to be known as "Torpedo Junction" during World War II. Merchant ships still stacked up there as they navigated the passage between the Gulf Stream and the Diamond Shoals, and they were easy targets in early 1942 for a pack of submarines that hunted there. Nearly 60 commercial vessels, including many oil tankers, were sunk and their crews killed off Cape Hatteras. British anti-submarine trawlers, as-

From the fully functioning Light-house, Park Service fact-finder Roger W. Toll could look north along miles of deserted beach, but during this 1934 trip he saw the Lighthouse's nearby oil house surrounded by drifting sand. *NPS, 1934*

sisted by reconnaissance aircraft, started making a difference that spring, and the surviving U-boats relocated to the mid-Atlantic to wreak havoc on convoys bound for Europe. While sharp-eyed watchmen looked for enemies out to sea, oil companies began searching the beaches for another kind of bounty. However, system-atic test drilling in 1944 to 1947 bore no oil. During the war years and the search for oil on the barrier islands, the North Carolina Cape Hatteras Seashore Commission and the Park Service made no progress on acquiring lands for their new project, and Congress extended the time for doing so another 15 years, to 1952.[15]

During Work War II, light vessel 105 had been recalled to serve as an examination vessel, and the shoals went unmarked. After the hostilities ended, shipbuilders painted *Diamond* on one more lightship, WAV 189 (later designated WLV 189), and sent her to coastal North Carolina in 1947. Measuring 128 feet in length and sporting diesel power, this ship was the product of Defoe Ship-building Company of Michigan, built for the U.S. Coast Guard. With this anchored ship and the skeleton light on Hatteras flash-ing a white light every 10 seconds, the Coast Guard assumed peace-time operations once again at Hatteras.

As early as 1943, Coast Guard officials had considered putting the brick Hatteras tower back in service again as a functioning lighthouse. It was in good condition, they reported, and its lens and operating mechanism were still intact. And the beach in front of the lighthouse was building again, not receding. By 1948, 1,000 feet of sand lay protectively between the lighthouse and the break-ers, the product of natural processes and beach stabilization ef-forts. Through a special use permit, the Coast Guard leased back the structure for 20 years and, with the Park Service, began prepar-ing the light for active service. Coast Guard officials planned to install modern lighting equipment, a Crouse-Hinds 36-inch du-plex rotating beacon. And they would put generators in the nearby oil house.[16]

During the post-War years, the lighthouse suffered from neglect and vandalism, especially the Fresnel lens. The Park Service and the Coast Guard tossed accusations of blame at one another while they painted, replaced windows, attacked rust, and upgraded the electrical service. The local population blamed the Park Service for the Light's condition, but the Coast Guard took responsibility and funded the necessary repairs in 1949, including the cost of a 6-foot chain link security fence around the tower and oil house. When the Lighthouse was re-lit in January 1950, there was little left of the original 24-panel symmetrical Fresnel lens that had helped warn ships at sea of the Diamond Shoals. Its remains were destined for a Park Service museum.

Although the National Park Service had been caring for the historic light station at Hatteras since 1936, the agency did not receive the much-anticipated donation of land for a national seashore preserve until 1953. Five years later, the Cape Hatteras National Seashore was formally dedicated, and 28,500 acres and 70 miles of shoreline were transferred by North Carolina to the Federal government. But it was a long, complex, agonizing process that pitted pockets of local residents against the Park Service. In 1950, the Seashore Commission was revitalized with new members, who were ready to proceed with land acquisition. The Park Service had secured private donations totaling $618,000 from Old Dominion Foundation and Avalon Foundation, managed by Paul Mellon and Ailsa Mellon Bruce, respectively, which equalled funding North Carolina had already identified for purchasing land.

In response to local opposition, the Park Service had decreased the size of the proposed recreational area to 30,000 acres. The agency omitted lands that had been built on since the original 1937 legislation, provided more room for expansion of the villages, and made boundaries conform better to land lines and suitable natural boundaries. Additionally, Director Conrad L. Wirth pledged to continue to protect the beaches in their "original, natural condition."[17]

In July 1952, the Park Service set up an office in Manteo on Roanoke Island for the purpose of acquiring land on the Outer Banks. Property must be surveyed, appraisers hired, and titles searched. Some acreage would be transferred to the Park Service from the state or from other Federal agencies. And many property owners within the boundaries of the new seashore park sold their lots as asked. But because of the magnitude of the program, numerous title anomalies, the difficulty in estimating property val-

The skeleton light tower was erected in 1935 to replace the threatened Hatteras Light. *NPS*

The Park Service made use of the two keepers' quarters during their management of Civilian Conservation Corps operations at Cape Hatteras. CCC workers repaired and renovated the buildings. *NPS*

ues, and the reluctance of some landowners to sell at what appeared to the Park Service to be fair market values, the Federal government placed all targeted properties under three blanket condemnation suits. When Director Wirth traveled to North Carolina in the fall of 1952, thousands of acres were still on the list of lands yet to be transferred. Money was running low, too. The Park Service asked the state to provide another $200,000. And Congress would be asked to support operations on the seashore over the next decade at an estimated level of $4.4 million.[18]

In a widely distributed open letter to the public and through a brochure, Wirth tried to answer questions and gain the confidence of island property owners. He assured them that their villages would not be taken, that their rights to fish and hunt would remain unviolated, and that just compensation for property would be paid. Wirth believed that the new recreational area would be a "fine opportunity for starting private enterprise in the villages, thereby increasing employment." The Park Service wanted no part in providing for the visitors' needs while they were on holiday. That—and the resulting economic benefit—was the residents' role. And he assured the property owners in the villages that:

> The National Park Service is keenly interested in continuing the program of control of beach erosion which was prosecuted with such success in the late thirties. The program will be resumed whenever funds are made available for the purpose after the lands have been acquired. In planning for the area, there must be, of course, a balance between provision of facilities for public use and service, on the one hand, and protection of the area from the ravages of wind and wave—and man—on the other. The two kinds of activity must proceed hand in hand.[19]

Many property owners contested the condemnation orders and hired lawyers. Sadly, the court cases were caught up in a shortage of judges and a backlog of cases, and delays stretched into the late 1960s, embittering many families. In dispute were approximately 6,000 acres. The fund established to pay the property owners, with interest, had also run dry. In 1969, Congress authorized monies with which to settle the outstanding cases and close this awkward early chapter of the Cape Hatteras National Seashore. Distrust of the Park Service would be harder to put to rest.

The principal keeper's house. *NPS*

North Carolina authorities responsible for managing coastal resources published a report in 1955 that served as a guide for state-wide coastal policy. The report's authors, prompted by recent damage from a trio of hurricanes, supported the ongoing work to stabilize the beaches and maintain the dune system on the Outer Banks, but they also advocated stricter guidelines for development and construction in these environmentally precipitous zones. When the bridge opened over Oregon Inlet in December 1963, visitors and the drive to develop the southern island villages surged over it down Highway 12 on its way to Hatteras village. Later that decade when officials once again grew concerned over the loss of beachfront on Hatteras Island and the impact of severe storms, they worried about more than historic lighthouses and villages populated by a few hardy families.

Hatteras was now a tourist destination and growing more popular each year. Motels, restaurants, and other businesses catering to the visitors' needs were built in view of sea, sound, and the black and white striped tower. The unincorporated villages had not adopted the zoning ordinances and minimum elevation requirements for new construction recommended by the state, but grow they did. And Dare County continued to oppose North Carolina's coastal zone management bill, written to protect natural resources and guide development in coastal counties. The County resisted the state's attempts to administer its lands and welcomed tourism as a means to distinguish the economy of the Outer Banks from the rest of the rural, economically depressed coastal plain.

To fortify the beach in front of Hatteras Light, the Park Service pumped over 300,000 cubic yards of sound-side sand to that location in 1966. The too-fine sand quickly washed away, and Park crews brought in sandbags. The U.S. Navy, which had operated a listening post just north of the lighthouse since 1955, asked the Army's Coastal Engineering Research Center to study the beach erosion that threatened 1,100 feet of shoreline at its installation. Based on a hydrographic survey and samples of the sea bottom out to 1,000 feet off the beach, the engineers recommended the installation of three timber sheet-pile groins stretching into the water 690 feet as the low-cost solution. When the groins, spaced 500 feet apart, filled with sand, the beach would be widened by 125 feet, the engineers predicted. While dismissing beach nourishment and restoration as too expensive to maintain annually, the report remarked that "early implementation of a beach fill and

Sand tracks served as roads. *North Carolina Department of Conservation and Development, 1937*

long-range periodic nourishment plan by the National Park Service and others within a reasonable distance would have considerable bearing" on improvements to the Navy's shoreline.[20] In 1969, the Navy followed the Corps' advice, but that activity targeted just one small stretch of beach. The Corps of Engineers listed 29 miles of Outer Banks seashore on its inventory of coastal properties that would need protection in the coming years.

During the 1970s, Park Service workers added more sand and small mountains of sandbags to its Cape Hatteras beaches, and, through its Denver Service Center, the National Park Service began formalizing a long-term solution to its erosion problem. In Denver, the Park Service had centralized its engineering and construction services experts, and it was this group that issued the first detailed report on the state of the Hatteras shoreline, in 1974. The thoughtful report reflected a new understanding of shoreline processes and encouraged managers to re-think the objectives that had guided the Park Service in recent decades as they watched the sea threaten the man-made resources of Cape Hatteras. The authors observed: "Contrary to the legislative mandate establishing the seashore, governmental agencies at all levels have been disrupting the natural processes of island migration functioning in the area and encouraging development of the village enclaves within the seashore." They went on to warn: "If this developmental philosophy continues, not only will the natural state existing along much of the seashore be destroyed, but the long-term survival of the barrier islands themselves may be threatened." Options for action ranged from taking no action that interfered with nature on its westward course to the mainland to taking aggressive steps to stabilize the beach and protect cultural resources. The authors of the report suggested that the agency also study the feasibility of moving threatened structures, including Hatteras Light, should protection in place become impossible.[21] In the spring of 1973, Cape Hatteras Superintendent Robert D. Barbee began informing state and local officials that the Service would no longer maintain a continuous barrier dune protecting Highway 12. The news was not welcomed and elicited media reports proclaiming that the Park Service was abandoning the islands to the sea.

Formation of the Outer Banks, according to coastal geologists' theories, dates back 12,500 to 4,000 years ago. They are part of the "coastal plain" that stretches from the Piedmont Plateau on the west to the Continental shelf on the east. Barrier islands usually mimic the shape of the mainland they buffer from the ocean, although that is not the case with the Outer Banks. And the North Carolina islands are further out to sea—20 to 40 miles—than other barrier islands off the U.S. coast. Hatteras Island has five ecological zones: beach, dunes, sandflats, maritime forest and shrub thickets, and tidal marshes. Although geologists may differ in their theories on how exactly the islands were formed during glacial and inter-glacial periods of uplift and submergence, they do clearly understand the dynamics of barrier islands and man's impact on those processes.

The combined actions of waves, winds, coastal currents, tides, and storms transport beach sediment, or sand—500,000 to 1 million cubic yards each year—from one location to another, achieving a balance between sand erosion and sand deposition. Ocean waters overwash the islands, and sound waters flood them from the other side. Vegetation helps stabilize the shifting landforms in a limited and sequential fashion. Wind direction, usually from the southwest and northeast, and currents dictate how the islands' shapes will change and where inlets will form, slowly or dramatically, depending on the results of hurricanes and major extratropical storms called nor'easters. Add to this a slowly rising sea level. Together these forces of nature are submerging the ocean side of Cape Hatteras National Seashore and building it on the landward side at an historical rate of about 5 feet per year. One marine scientist remarked that "the geography of the Outer Banks is in a constant state of change."[22]

Add the work of man to this dynamic mix of natural forces: roads that parallel the beach, bridges over inlets, ocean-front vacation homes, businesses built to support the tourist industry, and lighthouses. All built on a seashore that is on the move. Man has worked to protect what he has built on the Outer Banks. Evidence of groins, sandbags, mechanized sand transport, dredging, and artificial dunes can be seen along the beachfront, but a scientific understanding of the impacts of these efforts on the barrier island system has developed only in recent decades. For example, a well-engineered field of three groins will collect sand and widen the beach. But we know now that it also interrupts the natural flow of sand moving along the shoreline, resulting in flooding and sand erosion just south of those groins. For every action man takes

The last lightship to serve the Diamond Shoals represented a new design, one of six built for the Coast Guard. WLV 189 stood watch off Cape Hatteras from 1947 until 1966. She was later stationed in New Orleans, Delaware Bay, and Boston. *North Carolina News Bureau*

to halt the natural processes involved with barrier island migration, nature has a reaction that must also be reckoned with.Dirk Frankenberg of the University of North Carolina provides a comprehensive discussion of this topic with good illustrations in *The Nature of the Outer Banks: A Guide to the Dynamic Barrier Island Ecosystem from Corolla to Ocracoke*, published in 1995 by University of North Carolina Press. Visitors to the Outer Banks will find it a useful, readable field guide. Another useful volume is by Orrin Pilkey and his colleagues at Duke University: *The North Carolina Shore and Its Barrier Islands*, published in 1998 by Duke. It serves as a concerned citizen's guide to coastal management.

The National Park Service study of 1974 presented four new alternatives for how to manage a park built on a barrier island. Alternate strategy 1 demanded that man live with and adjust to natural events, much as had the early settlers on Hatteras. Natural processes would not be impeded. Overwash would be allowed. Structural control measures, like groins, would be banned. A transportation link, however, would be maintained. Such a policy meant the eventual destruction of man-made structures. The second strategy referenced the Park Service's standing policy for managing natural areas. The seashore would be faithfully preserved in a natural state. Dunes would not be re-built after storms. Man would not interfere with the natural process of inlet formation. The shoreline would not be "stabilized." Private property would not be protected by the National Park Service. Alternate transportation systems would be studied while opposing any expansion of existing roadways. And the Park Service should plan for the possible relocation or other disposition of all historic structures. Alternate 3 introduced nothing new to the status quo: continue partial stabilization and dune maintenance. Do nothing to oppose development. Work to save Cape Hatteras Lighthouse, or move it if it cannot be saved. The fourth strategy called upon the Federal government to purchase all the threatened lands and follow one of the first three alternates without concern for private or commercial interests. And finally, alternate 5 required structural shoreline stabilization measures to protect threatened areas, dune creation and maintenance, and private property protection.[23]

Duke University geologist Orrin H. Pilkey was one of many to respond to these environmental management alternatives. After reminding the Park Service that "migration" was a better term than "erosion" to describe what was happening to the beaches on Hatteras, he remarked that "Man insists on stabilizing an inherently unstable system," and that the first strategy described in the Park Service's report was the most ideal. Number 2, however, was acceptable and politically more feasible, he said.[24] The North Carolina Department of Natural and Economic Resources agreed that the second alternative, with some modifications, could be made to work, but warned that the first strategy abandons the citizens.[25] James Dunning, Superintendent of the Seashore, observed that the prevailing trend for managing the islands was based on controlling and stabilizing the environment to meet the needs of people. A new management philosophy was being called for that expected man to live with and adjust to the islands' natural processes. He predicted that the transition to this more environmentally aware outlook would have "consequences." Predictably, at public meetings held in January 1975, the attendees asked that the islands "be preserved just the way" they are now—alternate 3. Based on the Denver Service Center's work and the many reactions to it, the Superintendent and his staff sought to write an effective policy that addressed "the entire natural and social environment of the seashore—a barrier island environmental management policy," largely patterned from the second option offered in the Denver study.[26]

This proposed policy shift prompted a formal environmental assessment, required by Federal regulations. The Park Service was proposing that on its lands it would:

- Not stabilize the shoreline
- Assess inlet formation and closings on a case-by-case basis
- Allow natural processes to shape dunes, only intervening if human action threatened them
- Preserve viable transportation links along the islands[27]

An environmental assessment examines the affects that a proposed action—usually construction—has on the natural environment. But it also considers the possible impacts on cultural resources, the economy, transportation, and the people who live near by. It is a closely prescribed, lengthy, complicated process that calls for reviews by all levels of government and the public. The staff of Cape Hatteras National Seashore, under the leadership of Superintendent William A. Harris, spent most of 1976 describing more completely the conditions and environment of the Park before requesting in the spring of 1977 that a formal environmental assessment be prepared by the Denver Service Center.

The Park Service tackled the problem of how to protect the Cape Hatteras Lighthouse from the ocean as a task separate from the larger environmental policy work that was under way. In a 1980 report funded by the Park Service, MTMA Design Group, an architectural and planning firm, and North Carolina State University's Department of Marine Science and Engineering detailed six options:

- Take no action
- Relocate the lighthouse
- Build a revetment
- Build a partial revetment, install groins, replenish beach
- Install groins and replenish the beach
- Continue with beach replenishment alone[28]

Clearly, the Park Service would have to consider the ramifications of each option in light of its shift in environmental management policy to one of less intervention with natural processes. But the drive to preserve such an important regional icon was a strong one. Of the 1.8 million visitors to the Seashore in 1979, 21 per cent of them visited this landmark.

While officials grappled with protection options, nature continued her work. In response to storm action in 1980, the Park Service piled more sandbags on the beach and, as an emergency measure, extended the southern groin, which had been built originally by the Navy to protect its facilities north of the lighthouse. The shoreline had receded to within 60 feet of the tower and now completely covered the site of the original 1803 Hatteras Lighthouse. In a draft document that presented the Seashore's new general management plan, development plan, and environmental assessment for comment, Park Service specialists predicted that these temporary measures to protect the lighthouse would last only five years, at best.[29]

In 1982, an engineering firm studied relocating the lighthouse

to a new site 3,000 feet inland. Lee Wan & Associates of North Carolina, under contract to the Park Service, recommended moving the lighthouse in seven segments at an estimated cost of $5.5 million. Public response to all the protection options under consideration favored building a revetment, or protective structure, around the base of the lighthouse. Park Service officials agreed. It was amazing to marine scientist Orrin Pilkey and his colleagues that the revetment emerged as the preferred approach. "Not only did this choice contradict Federal and state coastal policy, including the 1978 Park Service decision to halt shoreline armoring, but the selection also contradicted the engineering and cost-analysis studies commissioned by the National Park Service." [30] The lighthouse would be surrounded with a concrete seawall coupled with a rock revetment and left as an island as the ocean inevitably moved in around it. In 1982, as the Park Service estimated the cost of that course of action at $6 million, maintenance crews brought in

The astronaut photographer aboard Shuttle mission STS-62 in March 1994 caught sight of the sediment built up off-shore from Hatteras Island. This image clearly shows shoaling off the island at the point where Hatteras turns to run east-west. *National Aeronautics and Space Administration*

more sandbags and even watched as artificial seaweed made from polypropylene was introduced in an attempt to slow down the rate of beach migration.

In 1983, the title of a Park Service resource management report captured the intensity of the problem: *"Coastal Erosion at Cape Hatteras: A Lighthouse in Danger,"* by Lorance Dix Lisle and Robert Dolan of the University of Virginia. Dolan's coastal geology research had been used heavily by the authors of the 1974 Denver Service Center report documenting conditions of the Seashore. These respected scientists predicted that the revetment planned by the Park Service would create an obstacle on the coastline that would prompt sand to accumulate north of it but starve the beach south of the lighthouse. Dolan and Lisle wrote: "This effect can already be seen with the three existing groins. The erosion of the first lighthouse site in 1980 was probably accelerated by these groins. The lighthouse will continue to affect the Cape Hatteras coast well into the 21st century." The scientists warned that without a major engineering solution at great cost, the lighthouse at Hatteras, as well as other historic seaside properties along the coast, would be destroyed.[31] Lisle and Dolan prefaced their report with a prediction, drawn from Percy Bysshe Shelley's poem "Ozymandias." The last lines read:

> Nothing beside remains. Round the decay
> Of that colossal wreck, boundless and bare
> The lone and level sands stretch far away.

Park Service officials, scientists, and the public agreed that it was worth the cost to prevent Hatteras Light from becoming a colossal wreck; they differed on how to go about doing it.

While the Park Service worked with the Corps of Engineers on modeling a revetment for the lighthouse, it took another stop-gap measure in 1983 when it authorized the Corps to improve the groin closest to the tower. A directive to extend the groin's length to 40 feet with a scour protection apron was signed by the Regional Director. Yet another interruption to completing the revetment planning came from engineer David C. Fischetti, who began an aggressive letter-writing campaign in favor of moving the lighthouse. He cited other examples of large structures that had been relocated and called for a more detailed engineering study of this option, which, of course, he could lead.[32] Fischetti enlisted the help of the Save the Lighthouse Committee, a group established

1852
1872
1917
1947
1975
1999

by developer Hugh Morton and supported by the North Carolina Travel Council. And the local Outer Banks Preservation Association was also attempting to coordinate support for preservation efforts. Adding its weight to the debate, the North Carolina Department of Natural Resources and Community Development went on record against seawalls and revetments. They do not protect beaches, they increase erosion along high-energy shorelines like Cape Hatteras.[33] North Carolina then enacted regulations prohibiting the use of all seawalls and other erosion control structures that harden the ocean shoreline.

Meanwhile, Park Service officials were still revising their general management plan and development plan for the Seashore. In 1984, options for preserving the lighthouse were still being pursued as a project separate from the management planning effort, but the amended draft of the plan certainly contained language that was pertinent. Park managers would:

- Control off-road recreational vehicles
- Expand ocean-side and sound-side visitor use sites
- Allow natural seashore dynamics to occur, except in

The changing face of the Cape Hatteras shoreline. *Computer visualization by Richard Cristin, based on Corps of Engineers data.*

The Corps of Engineers

The U.S. Army Corps of Engineers traces its roots to engineers who were a part of the Revolutionary army of George Washington. Separate engineer corps were established and retired in response to the young country's needs for assistance with constructing or repairing coastal fortifications during armed conflicts. Congress officially created a permanent Corps of Engineers in 1802 and expanded the organization's role in 1824 to include roads and canals of national importance. Army engineers supervised lighthouse construction from 1827 until 1910, and work along the coast included jetty construction, channel dredging, and other projects associated with coastal and inland waterway defense and commerce. Coastal erosion, flood control, and shoreline protection were added to the list of responsibilities in the 1930s. The Coastal Engineering Research Center, to which the National Park Service turned for help with its problems on Hatteras Island, was established in 1963.

For an informed discussion and good read, see Orrin H. Pilkey and Katharine L. Dixon's *The Corps and the Shore*, published in 1996 by Island Press.

instances when life, health, significant cultural resources, or transportation links along NC Route 12 were threatened
- Control spread of exotic species
- Prepare natural and cultural resource studies and action plans
- Cooperate with state and local agencies to realize the plan's objectives

The plan had grown increasingly bureaucratic, and, while language guaranteeing that the "dynamics of shorelines will be allowed to take place naturally" was still there, the list of exceptions and topics to study grew:

> Among those exceptions are historic zones where control measures if necessary will be predicated on thorough studies taking into account the nature and velocity of the shoreline processes, the threat to cultural resources, the significance of the cultural resources, and alternatives, including costs for protecting the cultural resource. Such studies must also determine if and how control measures would impair resources and processes in natural zones in order that management may make an informed decision on the course of action to be followed.[34]

Corps of Engineers staff completed their detailed engineering plans for a revetment around Hatteras Light in late 1985, months after North Carolina had passed regulations banning such structures. But there was a process in place for applying for exceptions to such regulations, and the Park Service and Corps still hoped to let a contract for the project in 1986. A team of consultants completed a comprehensive structural analysis of the lighthouse and defined a program for its preservation, and the Park Service was ready to act on its plan to build a revetment. But a steady flow of letters in 1985, 1986, and 1987 to high-profile politicians from respected engineers, professional movers, environmentalists, and scientists called for the lighthouse to be moved, not encircled.

Engineer Fischetti accused Cape Hatteras Superintendent Thomas L. Hartman of being seriously misinformed. Another letter-writer said that Hartman was responsible for distrust of the relocation strategy by local residents because he painted pictures of "bricks in the road" when he talked to them about moving the old tower.[35] Finally, in March 1987, Park Service Director William Penn Mott, Jr., asked for a review of the decision to build a revetment.

What Robert Barker, Southeast Regional Director, found when

he investigated the options for saving the lighthouse was strong regional opposition to moving it. Local residents feared that the 208-foot-tall brick structure could not be moved safely. Its demise would mean the loss of an historic landmark that was closely associated with the region and its people. The local economy was driven by the tourism industry; loss of the lighthouse was equated directly with loss of income. And would the historical integrity of the lighthouse be possible further inland?

There was another piece of "evidence" that had influenced decision-makers. In 1980, the Superintendent of Cape Canaveral National Seashore had asked an engineer at the National Aeronautics and Space Administration's Kennedy Space Center for his opinion on relocating the Hatteras Lighthouse. The engineer, in a two-page memo, outlined his concerns about moving the lighthouse, the sources of risk, and suggestions for mitigating those risks. He added that early estimates of $2.5 million to move it seemed "insufficient to accomplish the job." A cover note from a Park Service staffer suggested that the engineer "believes there are serious complications involved in moving the structure." He also said that NASA did not wish to be publicly identified with this project and considered this communication "informal." Park Service employees began referencing a "NASA study" that advised against relocation and persisted in relying on this as evidence in support of other options, as late as 1987. Another engineering statement that was widely circulated in support of the revetment option by Park Service personnel was from a retired U.S. Navy engineer, whose specialty was nuclear reactors. While well intentioned, neither document helped the managers make informed decisions, and they failed to impress the professionals who clamored for reconsideration of the relocation strategy.[36] The Director of the Southeast Region saw strong opposition to the revetment from coastal environmentalists and equally strong support of relocation from engineers and professional movers. In April 1987, he asked for help from a neutral source: the National Academy of Sciences' Na-

The remains of the original Hatteras Light (shown in the forground) would be covered by the ocean in a storm in 1980. *NPS*

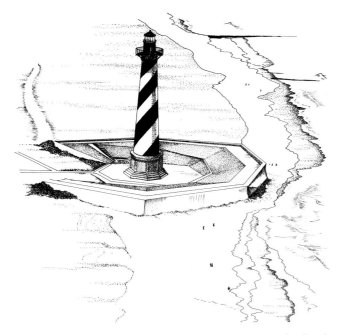

During the early 1980s, the Park Service favored protecting the Cape Hatteras Lighthouse with a seawall and revetment, which would allow the sea to slowly surround the tower and oil house, creating an island.
Drawing by Vince Wright

tional Research Council.

The National Research Council's Commission on Physical Sciences, Mathematics, and Resources appointed an interdisciplinary study team composed of members from four specialty boards: Environmental Studies and Toxicology, Ocean Studies, Marine, and Building Research. Nine experts represented the fields of coastal oceanographic processes, structural engineering, historical architecture, field ecology, environmental policy, and geomorphology of barrier islands. They began their comparison of options for protecting the Cape Hatteras Lighthouse in July 1987; a letter report was due in October, with a final study expected in April 1988.[37]

Not surprisingly, the academicians favored relocation over a revetment when they submitted their early findings that fall. While Regional Director Barker advised the Director of the Park Service that they should wait until they receive the final report before making a final decision, he proceeded with laying the groundwork for reversing the agency's direction, which included keeping Congress informed.[38] The Academy's published report, *Saving Cape Hatteras Lighthouse from the Sea: Options and Policy Implications*, was submitted on time. The scientists recommended moving the lighthouse, but incrementally. A move of 400 to 600 feet to the southwest would provide protection for 25 years, the report said, at a cost of $4.6 million. It would take one year to prepare for the move and 3 months to do it. And they suggested a method:

• Assess building structure
• Make minor repairs and reinforcements
• Tunnel the foundation and insert a series of needle beams
• Raise vertically with hydraulic jacks
• Lower onto roller resting on horizontal steel rail beams supported by concrete piles
• Move structure on tracks with hydraulic jacks, pulling it to its new location
• Place on newly constructed foundation

The authors scored this option as the "most reliable and involving the fewest risks. This scheme also rated well in terms of cost-effectiveness, preservation of historic and aesthetic values, and accordance with relevant public policies." Move the entire light station, they advised, so that "the entire complex could be preserved and its historical relationships to habitations and service structures left intact at a new setting." They believed that moving Hatteras Light would be an "exemplary response" by the Park Service to the generic problem of shoreline erosion.[39]

Park Service staff wasted no time preparing for the move. The Denver Service Center estimated its costs for providing design and construction services for the project. The Corps of Engineers agreed to perform the topographic survey and soil testing. And a site selection committee was organized to establish the precise location of the new foundation. Even though an environmental assessment for the new site was required, the team estimated that it could move the lighthouse to its new home in 1989. Superintendent Hartman advised that the length of the move be increased to 2,000 feet, providing the lighthouse with protection for 50 years. And he recommended the addition of a fourth groin to the existing 3-groin field to provide interim protection.[40] For $500,000, another groin might serve to protect the lighthouse for 2 years. By late that summer, the distance of the proposed move had stretched to 2,500 feet to the southwest, or 1,500 feet from the shoreline. Experts predicted that this location would provide 100 years of safety for the landmark. Cost was now estimated at just over $7 million. The Denver Service Center began working on formalizing the concept, and a draft environmental assessment was distributed for internal review in September. Park Service Headquarters judged the document not ready for public release. It was revised and resubmitted in February 1989 but not released for public comment until June. Obviously, the light would not be moved that year. More letter-writing campaigns were launched, this time by both local residents still vocally opposed to the idea and proponents complaining about the delays.

Based on the 1986 evaluation of the lighthouse's condition, the Park Service recommended preserving the structure before it was moved, and their consultants—Hasbrouck Peterson Associates with Wiss, Janney, Elstner Associates—drew up construction specifications for the job. The new site was staked out, and the Corps passed judgement on its ability to support the lighthouse. Added to the list of work that was needed before the journey could begin

In 1985, the Park Service sponsored a thorough study of the condition of the lighthouse. With scaffolding in place, Hasbrouck Hunderman, with Wiss, Janney, Elstner Associates, examined the entire structure and documented masonry cracks, metalwork corrosion, and other deficiencies.

International Chimney Corporation took the lead in restoring Cape Hatteras Lighthouse in 1991-1992. Improvements were made in advance of any long-term protection alternative being embraced by the Park Service, but the sand bags were a constant reminder that the sea was not far away.

were: a wetlands delineation along the path of the move, coordination with U.S. Fish and Wildlife Services, Section 106 historic preservation compliance, a new memorandum of understanding with the North Carolina Department of Cultural Resources and the Advisory Council on Historic Preservation, and an archeological survey, among other things. This work was all under way or being planned when the Superintendent of the Seashore wrote to the Regional Director, recommending that the relocation be put on hold.

Public comments to the environmental assessment were not favorable, Hartman pointed out. Elected officials were against the move. He believed that Congress would not support the project, now estimated at $8.8 million. Why not wait until the risks to the landmark were greater, he asked. The Southeast Regional Director concurred. He supported moving the lighthouse but would wait until the "threat of not moving . . . clearly outweighs the risk of moving." The Park Service would use the extra time to lobby Congress for the additional $3 million needed in funding and educate the public about the issue, he wrote in late 1989.[41] But there were many who already believed that the risk in waiting was too great.

While Park Service managers studied, lobbied, and assessed conditions, wind, water, and sand kept moving on Hatteras Island. And the maintenance crews kept piling up sandbags, repairing washed out footpaths and boardwalks, and wondering if the lighthouse would topple into the sea on their watch. Some planning work on the relocation effort continued. The environmental assessment was brought to closure, with a finding of no significant impact. In Denver, a request for proposals was issued for the design of the move, but the process was halted in the fall of 1991 with a "short list" of qualified bidders in hand. The Park Service did proceed with much-needed preservation work in 1991-1992 at a cost of $984,000. International Chimney Corporation of Buffalo, New York, in partnership with Wiss, Janney, Elstner Associates, evaluated the integrity of the structure, engineered instrumentation for long-term monitoring, replicated and refurbished iron, bronze and copper, restored brick and granite, and prepared the tall tower to face assault from the sea.

By late 1992, University of Virginia's Bob Dolan was seriously alarmed at the Park Service's inaction. Believing that storm activity would be especially severe that season, he contacted the Regional Director, who asked the Superintendent at Hatteras to activate a team to review conditions and develop short-term protection measures. The team recommended reviving the proposal to build a fourth groin to buy some time. In November, Dolan served on a committee appointed by the Southeast Regional office to estimate the risks to the lighthouse. In their report, the committee wrote: "Today, waves are actually breaking on the protective sand bags that have been positioned at the water's edge along the south flank of the lighthouse 135 feet from the base of the structure." Their advice was quite clear: "If moving is the NPS solution to the lighthouse problem, then this committee believes that time is of the essence. If the future of the lighthouse is to be assured, we recommend that the moving process be underway within 24 months, or by the fall of 1994."[42]

Because no actions were being taken at Hatteras, the Park Service re-programmed most of the funds previously authorized for the revetment project to conduct repairs at four other east coast seashore parks, leaving less than $800,000 for emergency stabilization measures. And the request to use those funds came in December 1992. Early the next year, the Southeast Region agreed to get help from the Corps of Engineers in designing a sandbag buffer and performing the engineering required on other interim measures, including a fourth groin. Another groin, to be installed 650 feet from the southern most existing groin, is an idea that was consistently championed and resurrected repeatedly by the Superintendent. The Park Service labeled these efforts "interim measures," while realizing that the groin would not even be designed for another two years. In thanking Barker for his support for emergency response funds, Hartman observed that now is the time to "pursue the long-term solution vigorously." In the case of the Park Service, "vigorously" meant another three years in which to plan, contract for, and actually move the Lighthouse, Hartman wrote.43 During the very active storm seasons of the 1990s, Park Service employees assigned to Hatteras Island defined "vigorously" in different terms, as they watched the fury of the sea scour the narrow strip of beach in front of the lighthouse.

The Corps and the Park Service dedicated precious time and money to designing and seeking approval for a fourth groin in 1994. And, not surprisingly, they got even more resistance to the proposal than they had a decade earlier. In 1996, the North Carolina Department of Cultural Resources and the Division of Coastal Management both refused to support any additional groin work. They told the Park Service that the time had come to move the lighthouse. Dolan predicted that a fourth groin would jeopardize the new site for the light station. But the National Park Service stubbornly sought legal guidance on how to request a declaratory ruling from the Coastal Resources Commission for an exception to the rules so that it could continue with its plans for installing the groin.[44]

Dolan and his colleagues spoke out often, trying to help the Park Service bring its plans for protecting the lighthouse to fruition. They wrote letters and reports, gathered more data, warned officials of the growing risks associated with doing nothing. In late 1996, Russ Berry, new Superintendent at Cape Hatteras Seashore, reportedly suggested that the Park could use help from North Carolina State University. Berry asked Marc Basnight, President pro tempore of the North Carolina Senate, who in turn asked the chancellor of the University to form an ad hoc committee to review and update, in a very short time, the National Academy of Sciences report on the Cape Hatteras Lighthouse. Early the next year, the University team added its contribution to the mountain of advice given the Park Service on this subject. The lighthouse must be moved, they said. That was the only option that was technically feasible. The report's warning was clear: move it soon—spring 1999—or see it destroyed.[45]

Momentum picked back up at the site of the proposed move and in Denver where the contracts to move it would be initiated; the Park Service was gearing up for a spring 1999 move, at last. Archeologists took to the field in the spring of 1997, and new managers at Cape Hatteras and at the regional office signed a project agreement that would guide their efforts: "All historic structures will be relocated into the same configuration relative to themselves and the coastline as now exists, and an eight acre area will be maintained as open space to approximate the historic scene. Additional major development at the new site will consist of a visitor information and orientation facility, toilet facilities and parking for 110 vehicles."

The price tag now read $12 million, and Congress had already approved the money needed for fiscal year 1998; 1999 funds were

pending. The Park Service issued a request for qualifications in 1997, looking for three to five companies with the unique set of skills required to safely move the tallest lighthouse in the United States 2,900 feet down the beach while the world watched. Six teams submitted their credentials in December 1997.[46]

In late 1997 and early 1998, local opposition to the move was rejuvenated and reinforced by elected officials. The Dare County Board of Commissioners sent a resolution to Congressman Walter B. Jones supporting the installation of a fourth groin to protect the Lighthouse.[47] Committees of concerned citizens and business associations banned together in their disapproval— and they wrote letters. In spring 1998, Senator Lauch Faircloth and Congressman Jones held a public comment meeting to hear their constituents' fears. Repeatedly, the new Superintendent at Hatteras, Robert Reynolds, and his staff were called on to provide information, defend their position, explain the mechanics of the move. In some public forums, retired former Superintendent Hartman was on the opposite side of the debate. Reynolds said that the Park Service acknowledged the "deep emotional attachment that citizens have for this icon of our national maritime heri-

With each passing decade, the Hatteras Light Station was closer to the sea.

tage." And he put the best spin he could on recent history:

> Interim protection measures such as groins, synthetic seaweed, sandbags, and even hopeful thinking over the decades have provided us with much needed time to seek the funding necessary to implement relocation. The National Park Service must pursue the option that has the best potential to preserve this important symbol for future generations. The best technical information available supports relocation as the option that will secure the structure for our children's children.

In the midst of coordinating a complex array of compliance issues and reviewing bid proposals, the Cape Hatteras staff also quieted rumors. No, the Lighthouse would not be sawed into three pieces. No, they would not be contracting with "Mom and Pop House Movers." The Park Service had no secret agenda.[48]   The "design-build" contract for the relocation was divided into two parts: detailed designing and planning for the move and the actual relocation. This two-part contract allowed for the design contract to be awarded using funding already in hand; the "construction option" could then be exercised when the rest of the funding was authorized by Congress. During the design phase, the contractor would provide a detailed technical plan for relocating the structure, to include blueprints, specifications, a monitoring scheme, a complete list of team members, and a project schedule. Of the six prospective bidders who had answered the call, a panel of Park Service and North Carolina State University professors judged two of them highly qualified.

Denver Service Center procurement officials issued a request for proposals to International Chimney Corporation and Emmert International in early 1998. They had 60 days in which to prepare their technical proposals. In May, the same Park Service-University team evaluated the proposals submitted by these two accomplished organizations and traveled to Buffalo, New York, and Clackamas, Oregon, for on-site presentations from the two bidders. Each was asked to submit a "best and final" proposal. The Park Service awarded International Chimney the job on June 19 and asked for the design package by October. The base award was $1,454,000; the actual move phase would cost another $8 million. After years of studies and delays, the Park Service was setting a brisk pace for the work at hand.

By the late 1990s, the southern-most groin built by the Navy in 1969 was seriously degraded.

International Chimney, the contractor responsible for the preservation work performed at Cape Hatteras in 1992, assembled an experienced team, which included Expert House Movers of Maryland. Together, these two companies had already moved three other lighthouses, and they intended to use the same methodology at Hatteras. Structural engineer David Fischetti was on board, as was Wiss, Janney, Elstner, who had already helped analyze the condition of the lighthouse and define a preservation program for it. In his initial proposal, Joseph J. Jakubik, project manager, wrote: "The ICC team is proud of our reputation with historic preservation and relocation projects. We recognize the importance of this project, and pledge full corporate commitments to the safe, successful relocation of the Cape Hatteras lighthouse."[49] Before the close of the year, ICC had secured the construction option, too. But even as the Park Service was awarding the contract, Dare County was still fighting the project. To halt work, the Board of Commissioners, along with some private citizens, filed a complaint and motion for a temporary restraining order, preliminary injunction, and permanent injunction in Federal Court. The Commissioners did not win their case, and the Park Service and International Chimney did not break stride as they arrived on site to begin their work in December 1998.

CHAPTER III

PREPARING TO SAVE AN ICON

"As the ocean stays in motion, eroding everything in its way, lighthouses
resting on sandy shores are facing the prospect of moving one way or another:
either inland, with the help of manmade ingenuity, or out to sea, in pieces."—
Seth Rolbein, "How to Move a Lighthouse in 15 Easy Steps," Yankee, April 1997.

The official request for proposals called for the relocation of the "structures of the Cape Hatteras Lighthouse Station, 2,900 feet south-southwest
in order to protect them from destruction. This effort will provide design development and construction documents and implement the construction work for this
move." [1] With the help of their colleagues from North Carolina State University,
National Park Service staff at the Denver Service Center evaluated the proposals
from International Chimney Corporation (ICC) and Emmert International on their
technical plans and their projected costs. High on the list of criteria for the technical evaluation panel were safety, preserving the integrity of the historic structure,
minimizing environmental impacts, and project management. [2]

For all the structures to be moved—lighthouse, both keepers' quarters and their
cisterns, oil house, and granite footings that once supported an ornamental fencing
around the tower—the contractors addressed four distinct phases: preparing and
stabilizing, lifting the structures from their foundations, transporting them to their
new locations, and securing them at the new site. The request for proposals had
outlined 25 separate project requirements that covered inspecting the structures
before and after the move, designing support and transportation systems, building
new foundations, providing tourist viewing areas, preparing the route over which
the buildings move, and returning the original site to a safe and natural condition.

Closed since November 22, 1998, the popular tourist destination became a construction site in December in preparation for the move.

In July 1998, International Chimney sent in their inspection team, led by Wiss, Janney, Elstner, to prepare detailed baseline drawings and to complete a thorough condition report.

Among the items in the scope of work was this piece of advice: "Schedule lighthouse move to minimize risk of exposure during move to nor'easters and hurricanes (late March to late May safest period for move)."[3] It was a project that required the participation of many partners and more than an eye on the weather.

International Chimney of Buffalo, New York, was established in 1927 to build smokestacks for steel mills and then expanded to providing chimneys for paper mills and other large complexes. The company diversified and began repairing and restoring chimneys and other tall structures, like bridges, parachute-training towers, church steeples, and lighthouses. According to President Richard T. Lohr, "The underlying theme to all International Chimney's business is tall structures and masonry." In 1989, ICC restored North Thatcher Island Lighthouse in Massachusetts. The lighthouse was on the National Register of Historic Places and demanded the accurate replication of historic materials. In 1992, ICC's crew traveled to North Carolina to restore Hatteras Light. On Block Island, Rhode Island, ICC and Expert House Movers joined forces in 1994 to relocate Southeast Lighthouse. They moved the 2,000-ton masonry lighthouse and keeper's quarters in one piece 360 feet. After the move, ICC helped the Coast Guard install a first-order Fresnel lens, which had been taken from Cape Lookout Light. After restoring the Cape May Lighthouse in New Jersey, ICC went back to Massachusetts and moved the 200-ton Nauset Lighthouse in 1996 and the Highland Lighthouse, which weighs 450 tons, in 1997.[4] "We've been practicing! May we be of service?" wrote Project Manager Joseph J. Jakubik in ICC's proposal to the Park Service.[5]

The concept for relocating Cape Hatteras Light, after it was cut loose from its foundation, was explained simply in ICC's initial proposal to the Park Service:

> Any relocation transportation system must deal with the act of lifting the structure off the ground, transferring the load to a transport system, moving the structure along the move route, and transferring the load of the structure from the transport support system to the new foundation.

The specific system ICC proposed using for this move had been employed by them and Expert House Movers three times before, twice on lighthouses and once to relocate a large radial brick chimney with an independent firebrick liner. Jakubik explained in the proposal that a steel support structure would be constructed under the lighthouse prior to lifting it to provide a rigid base. Frame and structure would be lifted with multiple hydraulic jacks linked together to provide a unified lift, and the inventor of the unified jacking system, Peter D. Friesen, would be on site. Data from sensors installed throughout the structure would ensure that the team maintained the support steel level in plane, cushioning the structure from differential stress.

Safely lifted, the lighthouse would move along the corridor to its new site on steel mats. Steel track beams would serve as rails, and roller dollies would allow the support frame to move along the rails. Three zones of hydraulic jacks would keep the tall tower aligned. And hydraulic rams, or push jacks, clamped to the track steel would push the support frame forward four to five feet with each push.

Wiss, Janney, Elstner Associates would be on hand to conduct a detailed condition survey of the lighthouse before any work was performed. Given their prior experience with the structure, they knew exactly where sensors should be installed to track any disturbance to existing cracks or repairs throughout the project. And structural engineer David Fischetti, with his many years of involvement and interest in the project, would provide expert consultation. Law Engineering and Environmental Services would conduct the very important geotechnical work required as they readied the corridor for the move, assisted by surveyors from Seaboard Surveying & Planning and civil engineers at Quible & Associates.

ICC claimed that they had demonstrated competencies in all the key areas. They had preserved and relocated large, historic structures. They had specific experience with the light at Hatteras and with the National Park Service. The team represented the various engineering disciplines required for the job. And they had corporate depth, resource capacity, and proven ability to lead a large

Official project photographer Mike Booher was on call to document flaws and capture details, including condition photographs of the interior.

48

It was necessary to take soil samples of the existing site, the corridor down which the lighthouse and other structures would move, and the new site as part of the geotechnical investigations. These data were used in the design of the new foundations and the engineering of the move road. Norwood Boyette, senior driller from Law Engineering, and Russ Wilkie of Lane Engineering drilled for samples near the lighthouse to a depth of 25 feet.

team.[6] The Park Service agreed. The technical evaluation and business evaluation teams gave International Chimney's proposal high marks. After considering the idea for over 25 years, the Park Service issued its notice to proceed with the preparatory work and design on June 19, 1998, so that Cape Hatteras Light Station could be moved to a safer site further from the crashing waves of the Atlantic.

Work commenced at Cape Hatteras on several fronts. While the primary focus of the media and tourists was on the lighthouse, other crews were clearing a wide swath from the new site to the existing light station and specialists from International Chimney began preparing the keepers' quarters and associated structures for their move south.   Skilled workers and laborers went from project to project on the job site, contributing their skills and expertise as demanded, always with the roar of the ocean in their ears and the shadow of the lighthouse across their path.

On three sides of the lighthouse, the ICC team dug a trench to the level of the original yellow pine timbers used by Simpson and Stetson to support the foundation, finding brick debris from the original construction as they dug. Lighthouse historians believed that the original builders had laid three layers of 4-inch by 6-inch pine; ICC found two layers of pine cut to random dimensions. With the granite base exposed below grade, Bob Simmons and Gabriel Tirado of ICC took deep horizontal core samples, so that International Chimney could verify the condition, weight, and composition of the granite. These borings were taken just below the line at which ICC intended to cut through the foundation and at locations where openings for the support steel would be cut.

Stetson's masons had constructed the Hatteras tower of two concentric brick walls, joined at intervals with radial brick masonry, but otherwise hollow in between. During their work, the 19th century crew had deposited an unknown quantity of brick rubble and mortar in the cavities. How much was there? And more importantly, how much did it weigh? To factor in this weight during their analysis, Wiss, Janney, Elstner employees drilled 1/2-inch diameter holes into the hollows and, with a borescope, determined the depth of the debris. From this measurement, they would estimate the lighthouse's weight.

With a hydraulic saw, Bob Simmons, of ICC's cutting and coring division, carefully cut one of three 8x8x4-inch sections of brick from the interior shaft of the Lighthouse so that it could be weighed and analyzed. The analysis would help determine what kind of materials should be used for future masonry repairs. ICC was extremely concerned about weight. The National Park Service had provided an estimated weight for the lighthouse: 2,800 tons. But ICC's calculations, based on actual field tests, brought the weight closer to 4,830 tons. Before lifting and moving the massive brick tower, ICC had to know how much it weighed.

ICC Chief Engineer George Gardner arrived at Cape Hatteras, drawings in hand, to launch the project. Gardner, who joined International Chimney in 1977, had overseen work at six other lighthouse projects along the east coast, and he was involved in the preservation of the Cape Hatteras lighthouse in 1992.

Alongside the modern wooden white fence that surrounded the lighthouse, crews started digging trenches in December 1998. Jeff Fellows and his ICC teammates exposed the monumental granite fence footers that had originally marked the perimeter of the light. Nineteenth century masons had laid

capstones of dressed granite on top of three courses of brick, which were supported by a mortared aggregate base of granite rubble. ICC numbered, or match-marked, each piece, documented its condition, and hoisted the 1-ton capstones from the trenches.

A brick walkway took lighthouse keepers of another era from the oil house to the tower's front door. Several layers of brick were laid on granite rubble. When individual removal with an electric jack hammer proved too destructive for the old brick—the mortar was still very strong—Jamie Markley and Richard Meekins of ICC resorted to sectional removal, cutting slabs seven bricks wide with masonry cutting saws. Framed and labeled, the bricks were trucked to the storage area in mid-January. Local house builder Richie Meekins was hired by ICC as a foreman for the Hatteras job, and he quickly gained a reputation as a "fixer" on the job when circumstances demanded a solution that wasn't reflected in the formal work plan.

Sections of ornamental wrought iron fencing, which had been fixed to the granite capstones, were also discovered in mid-December. Park Service Historian Rob Bolling was delighted with the resulting artifacts. According to the Lighthouse Board's annual report of 1871, the lighthouse had been enclosed by a "neat iron fence," which had long since disappeared.

ICC's long-time employee John Mitchell erected a scaling ladder up the south side of the lighthouse in late January, the first step in installing scaffolding.

John Mitchell wrapped scaffolding around the base of the gallery and cable around the ironwork under the lantern.

For its 2,900-foot journey, Hatteras Light would be equipped with automated sensors to measure several variables. The instrument package contained: 12 strain gages to monitor the transfer of load, 4 tilt sensors, 4 triaxial accelerometers to measure vibration, 3 extensometers to detect change of shaft diameter, and a weather station to track wind speed and temperature. Specialists from Wiss, Janney, Elstner, including Sun-Young Hong, shown above, began installing equipment and stringing cable—some 10,000 feet of it—inside and outside the lighthouse in January 1999. Richie Meekins of ICC helped with mounting exterior sensors to the side of the lighthouse.

A weather station was installed at the top of the lighthouse. Wind speed was of special interest! On March 3, the station recorded wind gusts of 90 miles per hour.

One of the screens from the computer program graphically displayed data on the lighthouse's tilt to a tolerance of 1/100th of a degree. ICC's plan allowed the lighthouse to tilt a bit, although a tilt of 15 degrees would have been safe. Just to be on the safe side, an old-fashioned plumb bob was also installed while the move was under way, hanging from the center of the tower and available for checking just inside the front door.

Daily on-site management of the large project was assigned to Dan McClarren, Park Service Facility Manager for Cape Hatteras National Seashore, and ICC Site Supervisor Skellie Hunt. On the job site and at partners meetings, they employed a no-nonsense management style that allowed them to get quickly to the source of a problem and find options for resolution. Paul Cloyd, Project Manager based at the Park Service's Denver Service Center, came to the Outer Banks monthly to run progress meetings to verify that the preparations and move were on schedule.

As the last of the brick walkway was being removed, ICC's John Mitchell, Cutting and Coring Foreman MikeVacanti, and Richie Meekins tackled the granite porch. The sides came off first, then the seven steps, the last two with difficulty. ICC discovered that the original stone masons had left shims of metal and granite in the steps and that the sub-foundation for the steps went all the way down to the timber mat. Marked and inspected, the porch, in pieces, was trucked to the storage area to await re-installation nine months later.

To cut the lighthouse free from its foundation, the ICC crew would excavate around the tower to the level of the pine timbers—below the water table. Drying the area was accomplished with a series of drain pipes connected to sump pumps.

Several components of the lighthouse had to be braced before the lighthouse was cut from its foundation. There were five courses, or rows, of monumental granite blocks, called plinths, that served as exterior facing at the lighthouse's base. Four were above ground; one was below. To discourage the top four rows from spreading during lift or transport, ICC prepared to brace them with galvanized steel beams. Unfortunately, ICC discovered that the base support beams just didn't fit. While waiting for replacements, they proceeded with the other braces and completed the job on January 28. They covered their work in plastic that windy, rainy morning. The plastic covers would protect the plinths during the sawing proceedure.

After excavating to the level of the pine mat, ICC brought out their heavy-duty diamond wire saw. Starting at a corner at 8:22 a.m. on Saturday, February 13, the 3/8-inch diamond cable had cut horizontally through 6 inches by noon.

Mike Vacanti checked the depth of the cut from the 200 foot long diamond wire saw.

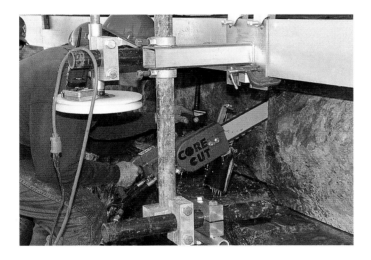

With diamond hydraulic chain saw, Mike Vacanti made vertical cuts to relieve the first of 36 exterior granite plinth stones.

These stones would be numbered and stored. On February 15th, the first pieces of granite stone, about 3 feet below plinth number 31, came free.

On the afternoon of February 17, plinth number 31 was removed. Number 30 came out the next day. The stones were numbered from the front door, working counter clockwise. Some stones still bore their original numbers, marked by stone masons 129 years ago.

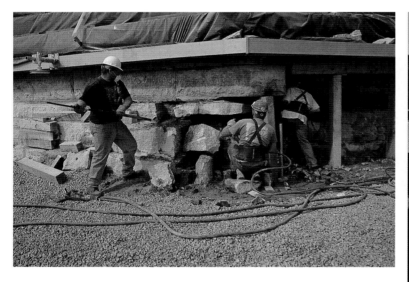

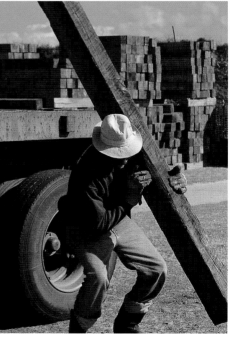

As rock was cleared to each new reach of four feet, Bob Hayes, Terry Barksdale, and Ben Heggie of ICC labored to shore up the newly exposed surfaces, while Joe Mason of Expert House Movers unloaded the truck.

Throughout the early months of 1999, ICC workers endured gale force winds and freezing temperatures to cut the tower from its foundation. Once the plinth stones were removed, ICC's men could supplement the cable saw with brute force to break out the interior foundation, which would not be saved.

The cutting and coring team, armed with hydraulic jack hammers, drills, and rock busters punched their way through the foundation of the lighthouse over the next 11 weeks. Ben Heggie and Robert Penfield, two of the local men hired by ICC, laid into jack hammers under the lighthouse. ICC's cutting and sawing group got its start doing bridge work, but they are called on regularly to cut through the foundations of lighthouses, chimneys, and other masonry structures.

The first task after the granite was removed, was to cover the pine mat with a steel mat which was made up of "I" beams welded together. Each orange shoring tower was built from four shoring posts braced laterally to form a tower 4 feet by 4 1/2 feet on center. In February, Terry Barksdale and Bob Hayes prepared 50-ton hydraulic jacks for each post. Jim Matyiko of Expert House Movers of Virginia and Richie Meekins man-handled one of the first towers into place, and Brett Yoho of Law Engineering followed with a torque check on all the bolts.

Shoring towers were placed directly underneath the lighthouse, on top of the steel mat, positioned jack end down onto the mat.

The light at Hatteras shone for the last time at 35° 15.3' north latitude and 75° 31.2' west longitude on February 28, 1999. With 12 feet cleared beneath the lighthouse, the light was turned off the next morning, with the move corridor clearly evident from the gallery. A red beacon now served to warn aircraft of the lighthouse's presence.

On April 1 at 11:25 p.m., Mike Vacanti reached the center of the lighthouse and discovered the tower's lead-encased grounding rod and a wooden surveyor's stake left by Stetson's men in 1869. Longtime ICC employee Vacanti, coring and cutting foreman, was always under the lighthouse with one eye on the schedule and the other on the job.

With the optimum period for the move fast approaching, ICC ordered night shifts as they tunneled their way underneath the tower, but it was difficult to find enough skilled manpower for this physically demanding, dirty work. They also started using a new tool that was added to the arsenal to speed the work—a jack-leg rock drill, usually reserved for heavy-duty mining operations.

On May 5, Cape Hatteras National Seashore Superintendent Bob Reynolds surveyed the last granite cornerstone left under the lighthouse. Four days earlier, ICC had reported that the lighthouse had tilted 2 3/4 inches, evidence that the load had shifted and that separation was imminent. When plinth number 7 came out at mid-day, the lighthouse was left on 34 shoring towers, each precisely placed and its jacks precisely pressurized according to the engineer's design. ICC had removed 334 cubic yards of granite debris from under the lighthouse in 81 days.

The team reflected on the important milestone they had accomplished and then began packing the cutting and sawing equipment so it could be returned to Buffalo, New York.

In addition to preserving the above-grade course of 36 plinth stones intact, ICC also cut the face from the course of granite blocks just below them. Pennfield and Mitchell's cut granite would be used as a veneer to face the upper portion of the lighthouse's foundation at its new location. After the face of each granite block was removed, a significant portion of the precision-cut plinth stone remained.

After ICC removed the last of the granite, Expert House Movers began installing seven 11-ton steel main jacking beams between the shoring towers. The 72-foot duplex main beams were pointed in the direction of the move. Experts's team ran 15 cross members perpendicular to the main beams at 4-foot centers. They adjusted the cross members to the bottom of the lighthouse, adding shims where needed to achieve a perfect fit. This system of steel served as the lighthouse's platform for the lift and move. Having checked the placement of each beam with a transit, Expert House Movers finished the job in late May by installing bright yellow strong back beams clamped to the main beams and the cross steel. 100 jacks supported the 7 main beams.

The lighthouse and 520 tons of support steel had to be lifted 7 feet to reach the grade of the move corridor and to allow installation of the transport system. The unified lifting scheme devised for the Hatteras lift called for 60 unified jacks, which were built into the main beams. Along with 40 common pressure helper jacks, this system controlled the lift. Redundant hydraulic hoses were run from the jacks to valved manifolds, which were connected to the unified jacking control panel.

The main unified jacking control board arrived on the scene in late May, along with Peter D. Friesen, its inventor. Brought up on farms in western Canada, Friesen entered the house-moving business in the United States as a young man. In 1955, he patented the Unified Hydraulic Jacking System; 20 years later, he popularized a specific use for that system. He divided the structure that was to be relocated into three hydraulic zones; within each zone, hydraulic jacks were connected together, creating the same pressure throughout each zone. With International Chimney and Expert House Movers, Friesen had used the unified system to move Highland and Block Island Lighthouses and Detroit's Gem Theater, the heaviest move on record using dollies. He would contribute the master's touch to the Hatteras lift, as well.

Manufactured by Jahns Structural Jacking Systems, the control panel, which itself weighed in at 36,000 pounds, became the center of attention—and training. Jerry Matyiko, owner of Expert House Movers of Maryland, studied the panel. Each of the 60 dials could control two jacks each.

Before the hydraulic jacks within the main beams could begin lifting the lighthouse, the load had to be transferred from the shoring towers. On June 4, the schedule called for the hydraulics to be activated on the two outer beams and the center beam, called pre-tensioning, the first step in the transfer of the load. But the seals on the right side of the unified jacking machine failed during testing, which prompted Bill Jahns to fly in from Illinois with replacement parts. Working through the night, Jahns and his sons replaced all the seals, and ICC's team was ready to try again.

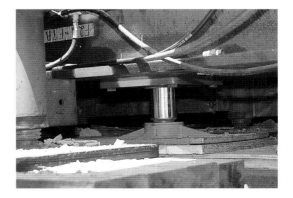

On June 5, just before noon, the pressure was slowly brought up on all the jacks in the unified system, and the Jahns celebrated. With much checking of gages underneath the lighthouse and adjusting of pressure, Expert House Movers achieved a balanced load and raised the lighthouse, less than 2 inches. The system worked; it was time for Lewis Fortt and others to remove the shoring towers and begin the lift in 12-inch increments.

Expert House Movers lifted the lighthouse incrementally over the next four days, achieving the desired height of 7 feet on June 9. After every unified lift, each jack, one by one, was depressurized, while keeping pressure on the surrounding jacks. Expert's Mike Landen, whose many specialties included hydraulics, measured to ensure that each lift was no more than 12 inches. The depressurized jack was retracted. Underneath the base plate of the jack, agile, strong workers quickly built towers of oak cribbing. When all jacks had been retracted and cribbed, they could be lifted in unison again. Jerry Matyiko of Expert House Movers had ordered 9,000 pieces of 6-inch by 6-inch by 4-foot cribbing for the Hatteras job, and they used it all!

With the final lift behind them, the lighthouse movers lifted their hats. But with hurricane season upon them, there was no time for lengthy celebrations. It was time to travel the corridor down the beach and away from the waves.

*The sun will never rise
again on the lighthouse
at its original site.*

CHAPTER IV

ABANDONING THE OLD SITE

We do what we can to preserve historical landmarks in their original positions, but Mother Nature always has the bigger hammer.
Paul Cloyd, National Park Service
Extrapolations Magazine, Purdue University, Spring 2000

Before the lighthouse could be relocated to its new home, International Chimney had to build a reliable path to the new site and relocate the oil house and the two keepers' quarters. The National Park Service selected the new site for the light station with care: 2,900 feet, more than half a mile, to the south-southwest would place the lighthouse 1,600 feet from the ocean's reach and, barring no cataclysmic storms, provide protection for more than a century as Hatteras Island continued to migrate toward the North Carolina mainland. Most of the proposed move corridor had been cleared or built upon in the past. The last 400 feet, however, were covered by typical maritime thicket that prospered behind the protection of dunefields. Red cedar, groundsel, marsh elder, and yaupon holly grew densely there, the decay of their leaves working their way into the layers of the soil. Blowing salt air killed and shaped the tops of those trees, but the resulting canopy provided an almost impenetrable network of branches that kept the salt air from reaching the plants below. The organic-rich soil produced a complex community of plants, as International Chimney Corporation's team soon discovered.[1]

To design a pathway that would accommodate the 4,830-ton tower, Law Engineering and Environmental Services and civil engineers at Quible & Associates started with the geotechnical data prepared by the Army Corps of Engineers in 1989. The conditions along the route were generally uniform, consisting of fine sand with loose to medium densities in the upper 10 to 20 feet and much denser below that depth. Thin surface pockets of sand with silt or clay were present in low areas. As part of their exploration, Law bored into the soil to depths of 25 feet in the previously unexplored areas of the corridor. Elsewhere, they used standard penetration testing, taking soil samples every 30 inches along the corridor until dense sand was discovered and every 5 feet thereafter the entire length of the corridor. In addition, Law used a dilatometer, an instrument that measures thermal expansion below ground, to document the soil's settlement behavior at 200-foot increments along the route.[2] With this data, the engineers designed a level, sound road down the beach on which the lighthouse would be pushed during the summer of 1999.

The entire corridor, 100 feet wide, was cleared of vegetation and preexisting pavement. Crum Construction, ICC's site work subcontractor, rough-graded, proof-rolled, graded again, and compacted the sandy soil.

A maze of thicket stood at the light station's new site, 2,900 feet to the south-southwest.

Looking from the gallery of the lighthouse, the project team could see the proposed move corridor, which included a parking lot for beach visitors, which would have to be demolished.

In January 1999, chain saws and chippers made quick work of the thicket, and root rakes cleared the remaining brush. Much of the soil in this area, rich in peat, would not compact well enough for the roadbed, and it was removed and replaced with suitable fill.

As Crum Construction, a local Outer Banks company working for ICC, began building the lighthouse's highway in the sand in late January, the move corridor became clearly visible from the air.

Seaboard Surveying and Planning's employees were on site at the lighthouse and along the move corridor. The Park Service required that the tower and its associated buildings be in the same locations relative to one another and the sea at the new site as they had been at the original site, both in lateral measurement and in elevation. The move corridor was also precisely laid out. All this work required frequent readings from the surveyors.

The first piece of news that the surveyor delivered to the Park Service was that the lighthouse was not 200 feet tall as believed for over a century. Instead, it is 198 feet tall.

Once the corridor was rough-graded, Crum ran proof rollers over the sand to search for soft spots and pack them down. The contract required them to make four passes, the last two perpendicular to the first. Vibratory rollers completed the mechanical compaction of the sand. When the roller made two passes without detecting any problem areas, Andy Bick (right) and Bob Medford (left) of Law Engineering performed deep soil compacting tests to verify construction progress.

After the keepers' quarters and other structures had been safely relocated to the new site, the corridor was flooded in April. Frequent rains had created more water around the excavations at the new site than the drainage system could carry away. To drain the area, the ICC team pumped the water into the move corridor, where the weight of the water helped compact the new roadway.

Crum drained the temporary lake in May and added crushed stone mixed with lime, called "crush and run," to the sub-grade, which also had to be compacted to the proper density and tested. By June, all was ready for the lighthouse at the north end, while crews still labored to complete the roadway at the new site.

When the new site was cleared and graded, ICC built a foundation for the lighthouse. But instead of timber mats, International Chimney built a foundation of reinforced concrete. ICC Chief Engineer George Gardner and consulting engineer Dave Fischetti designed the foundation to accommodate the stresses of the lighthouse as it traveled across it during installation and as it rested in place for the next century.

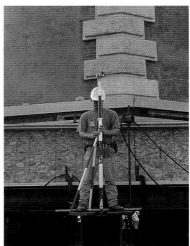

Precision location and soil tests for the new lighthouse foundation site were critical. John Mayne of Seaboard Survey, who came to be known as "the Navigator" on the job site, took readings to ensure that the relationship of the tower to the rest of the relocated station was consistent to within 1/10 of a foot. Assigned by Law Engineering as their on-site liaison, skilled technician Brett Yoho tested the soil at the relocation site.

Crum Construction started excavating the new foundation for the lighthouse on April 5, ICC crews built the forms required for pouring the 4-foot deep 60-foot by 60-foot base. S. T. Barnes installed epoxy-coated steel rebar—59 tons of it—in 3 inch grid patterns, with Law Engineering's Brett Yoho looking continuously for flaws.

Coastal Ready Mix Concrete Company started mixing and delivering concrete before dawn on May 1, and S. T. Barnes began pouring. They poured for 4 hours, for a total of about 550 cubic yards. Law Engineering took "slumps," or samples, from every other truck, which would be cured off site and tested to ensure that the concrete would meet the 4,000 pounds-per-square-inch (PSI) design requirement. In fact, it exceeded it. At 5,000 PSI, no stress or heat cracks were ever found in the laboratory.

The small brick oil house built close to the base of Hatteras Light almost goes unnoticed in photographs of the tall lighthouse. But a well-used brick sidewalk connected the two for the convenience of the keepers who had to carry a supply of oil from the storage building to feed the lamps. When the lighthouse was converted to electricity in 1934, two generators and a bank of batteries were installed in the oil house. In 1950, when Hatteras Light was put back in service, the Coast Guard stowed emergency generators in the small outbuilding. It was the first structure moved in 1999 as International Chimney and Expert House Movers prepared to relocate the Light Station. It would also be the last structure set in its final new location.

After the brick floor of the 16-foot by 8-foot structure was removed in early February, Mike Vacanti, cut 16 openings at the base of the building, into which steel beams and oak cribbing were slid. Braced and banded, Expert House Movers lifted the structure approximately 7 feet with unified hydraulic jacks placed under the move beams. At that height, they inserted rocker beams perpendicular to the main beams and rolled two sets of rubber-tired dollies under them. With a tractor, the team trucked the oil house to the perimeter of the new site for storage on February 5—the first structure to move from the station.

Cape Hatteras Light required the attention of three keepers to ensure that it remained lit without disruption each night and was well maintained. To house the principal keeper and his two assistants, and their respective families, there were two keepers' quarters at the station; a double assistant keepers' building to the left above and the principal keeper's quarters to the right.

In the interest of historic preservation, even the cisterns were saved. Three 5-foot-deep brick cisterns provided rain water storage for the keepers and their families, two at the double keepers' quarters and one at the principal keeper's quarters. Structurally, they were not part of the living quarters and were moved separately. While excavating around the cistern at the double keepers' quarters, the contractors unexpectedly found a 500-gallon tank full of diesel fuel and water. With Park Service's assistance, the crew disposed of the potential hazard.

The eastern cistern of the double quarters, shown here, measured 14 feet by 13 feet. After excavating by hand around each cistern, ICC cleaned and banded them, inside and out. Expert's crew placed cross steel beams under the cisterns at 6-foot intervals and inserted main lifting beams under the cross steel. With at least 4 jacks in place under the main beams, the movers lifted them high enough for flat bed trailers to be backed under them. By February 10, the cisterns had been moved to the new site.

The white wooden frame quarters at Hatteras Light Station was built large enough for the two assistant keepers and their families. Constructed first in 1854, modified and enlarged to its current configuration in the 1890s, and renovated several times over the decades, the double keepers' quarters is a two-story structure, 66 feet by 20 feet. It has a single-story addition, 23 feet by 14 feet, a full-length front porch, and 2 chimneys. For many years, the National Park Service had used the double keepers' quarters for a museum and interpretive center, but as late as 1952, visitors to Hatteras Island could rent the quarters. A room with access to a bath plus meals on the "American Plan" at the Cape Hatteras Lighthouse Lodge in 1952 was advertised at $4 a day per person, while a two-room furnished apartment with private bath, linens, and cooking facilities ran $30 a week.

After excavating around the structure, International Chimney examined the masonry piers that supported the building and determined which of the "historic" bricks they could save to re-use as above-grade facing material at the new site. The excavations had to extend some 70 feet east of the building to give Expert House Movers room to maneuver the main lifting beams under the house.

The single-flue and double-flue fireplaces of the building were constructed along the longitudinal center line, and they were braced in January 1999 in preparation for relocating the quarters to the new light station site. First-floor windows and doors were also braced. The long front porch would stay attached during the move.

The movers built cribbing towers to support hydraulic jacks, which took the weight of the building after the team cut through the existing masonry support piers in February. They inserted 3 main steel beams and 13 cross members to support the large house.

On February 22, with 30-ton jacks, Expert House Movers lifted the structure in 1-foot increments until they reached approximately 7 feet. At this point, they installed rocker beams under the main beams, under which two sets of rubber-tired dollies with integral hydraulic jacks were placed, with Jim Matyiko of Expert House Movers of Virginia watching the progress.

With a tractor, the quarters were moved out of the excavation and down the sand track on February 25. In less than 2 hours, it made the trip. A month later it was placed on its new foundation. In June, it was mated with its cisterns and sported new masonry piers.

Stetson constructed the masonry quarters for the principal keeper in 1870 from materials left over from the lighthouse construction. Built on piers, the original L-shaped house was filled in with a wooden frame addition, bringing the measurements of the quarters to 35 feet by 33 feet. It had two porches and three chimneys.

Before the principal keeper's quarters could be moved, in January ICC braced all its first-floor windows and doors, and Clyde and Alan Scarborough carefully protected the slender chimneys from lateral or horizontal movement during the move. Crews excavated to a depth of approximately 3 feet to expose the original footings of the house. Employing a traditional method for relocating structures, in early February, the ICC team penetrated the foundation below grade with diamond-toothed hydraulic chain saws, supporting the structure with temporary screw jacks and cribbing. The wooden frame addition to the house made the job of accessing all the foundation points more difficult. ICC crews used hydraulic drills to chip away at the original masonry. When the cuts were all made—more than originally planned—the team inserted two steel main beams and cross members at 4-foot centers to support the frame.

With steel in place, the structure was lifted 2 feet off the ground with a unified jacking system on March 17. Expert House Movers' team continued to raise the house until rubber tired dollies with hydraulic jacks could be placed under the main beams. The first attempt to roll the principal keeper's quarters from its excavation was thwarted by heavy equipment problems. Unfortunately, while the crew took time out to solve the mechanical problem, cribbing and one jack apparently settled, causing a minor crack under one of the windows, which ran down to the foundation.

By late April, the new site was starting to resemble the original light station, with the two quarters in place and the lighthouse foundation under construction. Only the lighthouse remained at the old site, waiting its turn.

On March 23, Expert's equipment pulled the keeper's house from its site and slowly towed it south.
New foundation piers were built for the principal keeper's quarters, and the building was installed on its new piers on March 24.

This photo, taken March 24, 1999, with the tower still at its original site, shows the keepers' dwellings and the other outbuildings already moved.

Jerry Matyiko, a Richmond, Virginia, native, established Expert House Movers of Maryland in 1973. Relying on expertise he gained by working with his father and with the Navy, he had begun raising buildings for a living in the 1960s. Partnering with International Chimney, the family business, headquartered on the Eastern Shore of Maryland, had moved two other lighthouses before the 22 Matyiko family members and other employees arrived at Cape Hatteras. Expert House Movers' long list of accomplishments includes the relocation of the Shubert Theater in Minneapolis, the GEM theater in Detroit, a 135-foot brick chimney for Corning Glass in Pennsylvania, and the

Third Haven Quaker Meeting House, the oldest documented building in Maryland. Jerry Matyiko was known to be a tough guy who took on difficult jobs. With a cigar as his constant companion, he led by example. There was no task too hard or too menial; if it needed doing and he was there, he did it. And he expected the same of everyone else on his payroll.

CHAPTER V

MOVING THE LIGHT

Failure to sucessfuly move the lighthouse simply wasn't an option, not when you do something with as much scrutiny as the Park Service provided, when local residents showed such concern and when there's so much national and international publicity. Everyone was watching.

Randy Knott, Law Engineering
Georgia Tech Magazine, Fall 1999

Visitors to Cape Hatteras National Seashore during the spring and early summer months of 1999 stood at the bright orange security fence surrounding the lighthouse project and speculated about how the tall tower would be moved. Among the ideas offered were rolling it on its side, cutting it in pieces, floating it down the flooded corridor, and pulling it on a sled down the sand. In fact, it would be pushed.

The lighthouse comes to rest at its new site.

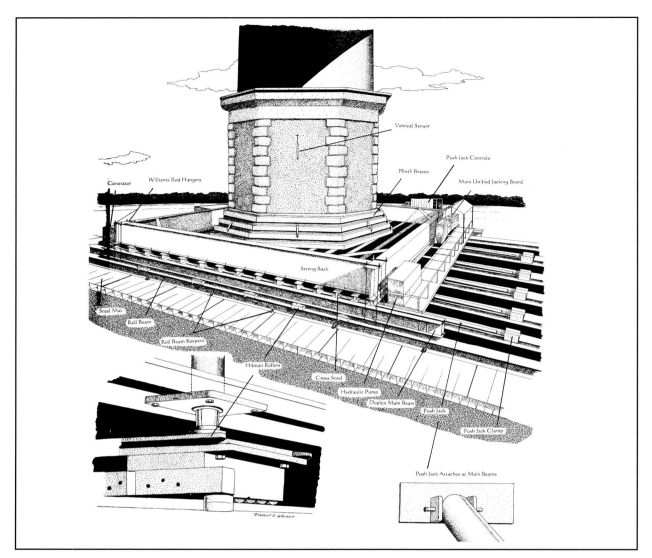

Labels in illustration: Vertical Sensor; Push Jack Controls; Plinth Braces; Main Unified Jacking Board; Generator; Williams Rod Hangers; Strong Back; Steel Mat; Roll Beam; Roll Beam Keepers; Hilman Rollers; Cross Steel; Hydraulic Pump; Duplex Main Beam; Push Jack; Push Jack Clamp; Push Jack Attaches at Main Beams

Vincent E. Wright

Cape Hatteras Lighthouse on the move. *Drawing by Vince Wright*

After the International Chimney team lifted the lighthouse from its foundation some 7 feet, it was standing on cribbing towers. Expert House Movers once again employed shoring posts under the main beams and the cross supports and depressurized and retracted the jacks one last time.

Hours after the lighthouse reached the desired elevation on June 9, Expert's crew was installing guide beams under the structure, along which travel beams would be inserted—one continuous line of travel beams under each of the seven main beams. These travel beams, in place by June 15, would serve as the track down which the lighthouse would be rolled.

Next the movers mounted heavy-duty steel roller dollies under each of the jacks built into the main beams. The rollers, attached by plates to the jacks, rested on the travel beams, kept in place by customized guides. Each Hilman roller, being inspected here by Mike Landon, weighed in at nearly 250 pounds. They would serve as the lighthouse's "wheels." The jacks, functioning as a common pressure system divided into three zones, would keep the lighthouse level as it was transported to its new site, isolated from stresses that could damage the masonry structure. Landon, skilled at all the trades that Expert House Movers needed on the job, was also the company's hydraulics expert.

In front of the lighthouse, in the direction of the move, Expert House Movers laid welded H-beam matting, covering an area 72 feet wide by 80 feet. They positioned another set of guides and travel beams on the mat, aligning them perfectly with those under the lighthouse. Geri Ellen Matyiko, daughter of owner Jerry Matyiko, and Mike Landen gave the beams a good coating of lubricant—Ivory soap—so that the Hilman rollers would ease down the tracks.

Hydraulic rams were used to push the 4,400-ton lighthouse and 430 tons of steel.

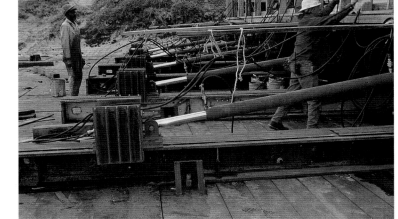

"Behind" the lighthouse, on the side opposite the move direction, the travel beams extended from beneath the structure approximately 10 feet. They were supported by oak cribbing to match the height of the elevated tower. Onto the exposed end of each of the five inner beams, Expert House Movers clamped a hydraulic push jack—a jack on its side, so to speak. They attached rams to pivot plates at each main beam and joined jack and ram. The push jacks would be activated in a unified push of the rams for 5 feet, moving along the travel beam against the combined weight of the lighthouse and its hefty steel carriage. The lighthouse, in turn, would roll along the travel beams a distance of 5 feet with each push. After the push, the jacks would be disconnected, the rams retracted, the jacks moved forward along the travel beams, and the system recharged for the next push. This was the same strategy International Chimney and Expert House Movers had used to move the Block Island Lighthouse in the early 1990s, but they were working with improved push rams at Cape Hatteras—and a much bigger lighthouse.

The lighthouse left behind 9,000 pieces of oak cribbing. Each 58-pound timber was handled approximately 18 times during the project, for a total of more than 9 million pounds!

During the months of preparation for the move, there had been steady interest from the media. Bob Woody, Public Information Officer for the Park Service at Cape Hatteras, had held regular press conferences, opening up the site for supervised photo sessions and interviews. But as "move day" drew nearer, media interest grew, and the story captured international attention. Satellite trucks started arriving on site on June 14 to provide live broadcasts, and network television personalities joined journalists from local weeklies to capture the story and share the lighthouse's progress with the world. Some 200 media representatives registered with Woody to cover the story over the course of the project.

In a light rain and in the focus of the media, with 10,000 onlookers, International Chimney and Expert House Movers began pushing the Lighthouse down the beach on June 17 at 3:05 p.m. It went 5 inches and stopped. The first pushes were systems checks, and all systems were reported "go." They went another 10 feet and stopped for the day. Witnesses had to look very intently to see the tower move, but the proof lay in exposed mat, cribbing, and beams on the aft side of the tallest lighthouse in America.

Bob Woody

Gil Hollingsworth, WRAL-TV photographer, explaining the project to visitors on the sidelines.

On the second day of the relocation, the lighthouse covered a respectable distance of 72 feet. In advance of the moving lighthouse, men labored to lay mat and travel beams in its path, picking up gravel and materials from the ground just covered and transporting them to the forward side. The movers orchestrated this leap-frog motion down the beach corridor for 23 consecutive days. The first equipment problem to hamper the move was a broken Hilman roller on Day 8, but it was removed in 15 minutes. The transport system had been designed with a redundancy factor that allowed for equipment failures while still maintaining the integrity of the design—and the safety of the lighthouse.

The view from the top on June 25—looking ahead.

Jerry Matyiko, President of Expert House Movers, studied the unified hydraulic control board. From here, the operators would control the push rams.

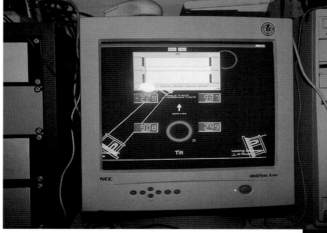

Everyone wanted to be able to say that they had pushed the Cape Hatteras Lighthouse, and Duke University Professor Orrin Pilkey, a long-time proponent of moving the structure, took his turn. The controls were housed in the back of a work truck, which kept pace with the lighthouse near the push rams.

On Day 12, the monitoring system that measured the vertical attitude of the lighthouse gave some alarming readings. The tower was reportedly tilting by 8 feet! The job shut down, but with level in hand, Brett Yoho of Law Engineering and ICC Project Manager Joe Jakubik just couldn't agree with the finding. They installed a plumb bob the next day as an added precaution.

The movers worked efficiently and steadily down the path. They could accomplish a single cycle of pushing and resetting the rams in 7 minutes, as demonstrated by Geri Ellen Matyiko. On Day 13, they reached the half-way mark. Their best day was 355 feet on July 1, and an audience was always lined up at the fence.

In early July, Lewis Fortt, skilled with the cutting torch and any other tool Expert gave him, took time out to make a repair. While rollers and jacks occasionally failed, a greater impediment to progress was the steady flow of VIPs and media who gained access to the site. While the team appreciated the interest and the compliments on a job well done, there were days when the attention was detrimental to the schedule.

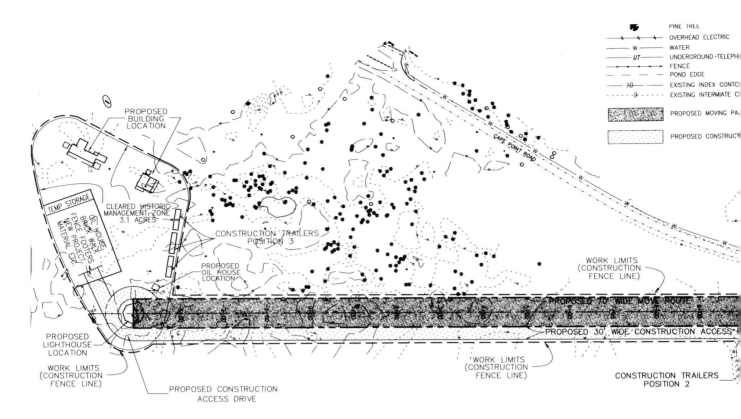

PROPOSED BUILDING LOCATION

CAPE POINT ROAD

CLEARED HISTORIC MANAGEMENT ZONE 3.1 ACRES

TEMP STORAGE

OIL HOUSE
BRICK WALK
FENCE FOOTERS
NEW PROJECT
MATERIAL EDGE

CONSTRUCTION TRAILERS POSITION 3

PROPOSED OIL HOUSE LOCATION

WORK LIMITS (CONSTRUCTION FENCE LINE)

PROPOSED 70' WIDE MOVE ROUTE

PROPOSED LIGHTHOUSE LOCATION

WORK LIMITS (CONSTRUCTION FENCE LINE)

PROPOSED CONSTRUCTION ACCESS DRIVE

PROPOSED 30' WIDE CONSTRUCTION ACCESS

WORK LIMITS (CONSTRUCTION FENCE LINE)

CONSTRUCTION TRAILERS POSITION 2

Civil engineers at Quible & Associates prepared this general site plan (above). It details the original site (right), the move corridor, and the new site (left). On this drawing, the lighthouse relocation team plotted where construction trailers would be positioned, materials stockpiled, fences built, and access roads built.

< As seen from the top of the lighthouse on Day 5, the original pine timbers upon which the base of the tower was built lay exposed.

> On Day 8, National Park Service pilot Bob Trick took the official photographer for a look at the progress that had been made.

DAY 3	DAY 7	DAY 12

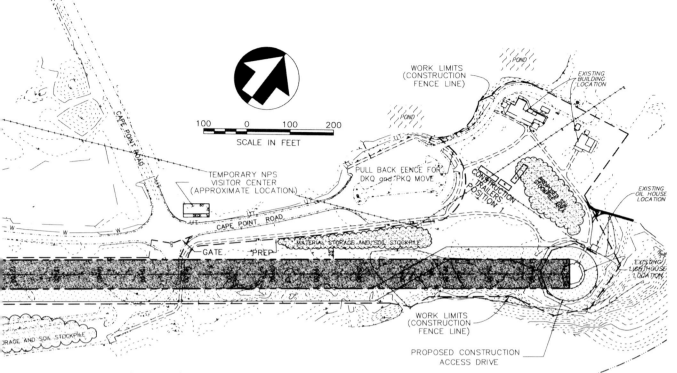

TRACK RECORD

Day	Date	Moved (ft)
1	06/17/99	10
2	06/18/99	72
3	06/19/99	19
4	06/20/99	24
5	06/21/99	60
6	06/22/99	136
7	06/23/99	135
8	06/24/99	219
9	06/25/99	223
10	06/26/99	174
11	06/27/99	108
12	06/28/99	98
13	06/29/99	288
14	06/30/99	204
15	07/01/99	355
16	07/02/99	122
17	07/03/99	25
18	07/04/99	0
19	07/05/99	252
20	07/06/99	221
21	07/07/99	76
22	07/08/99	0
23	07/09/99	76

DAY 19	DAY 21	DAY 22

90

On Day 23, July 9, the International Chimney-Expert House Movers team covered the remaining 76 feet. After the last push, the team lifted a toast in celebration of the final milestone in a 2,900-foot journey. Cape Hatteras Light was officially "landed" at 35° 15' 1.92" north latitude and 75° 31' 43.74" west longitude at 1:23 p.m.

Shoring towers and cribbing were quickly installed under the lighthouse and travel beams removed. On July 15, the tower was lowered 11 inches and, over the next two days, adjusted to reach the exact elevation prescribed for this official aid to navigation. Surveyors calculated the height of the center of the beacon to be 192.2 feet and the spire of the lighthouse to be 210.01 feet. Expert removed the steel carriage that had supported the historic structure so well, transferring the load once again to shoring towers.

On Day 22, MikeBooher photographed this scene of the lighthouse's final postion, from the top of the tower.

During the last days of August and early days of September, Hurricane Dennis visited Hatteras Island and stalled off the coast. While the rains flooded the site and the ocean swept into Buxton taking out roads, the lighthouse stayed rooted in place. The weather station mounted at the gallery level was damaged, with the last wind speed being recorded at 128 miles per hour. All but two of the lighthouse's landing windows were blown in. For several days, access to the light was possible only by raft. Hurricanes Dennis and Floyd, which threatened to follow, served to remind the Park Service—and the world—why the lighthouse had been moved away from the ocean's edge.

National Park Service Superintendent Bob Reynolds, with Foreman Jeff Spurgeon of Masonry Building Corporation looking on, helped lay some of the first bricks under the lighthouse. The professional bricklayers from Masonry Building Corporation laid some 145,000 bricks to fill the void.

The granite plinth stones, which had been cut from the below-grade course months earlier, were assembled near the lighthouse in mid-August. By early October, after the braces had been removed from the lighthouse, they had all been carefully installed, followed by the steps. *Mary Basnight photo*

The International Chimney team spent three months finishing their work at both sites. While the lighthouse was being restored to its original external appearance, Expert House Movers moved the oil house into its final location and packed their tons of gear and materials for the trip back home.

On the evening of November 13, 1999, Cape Hatteras Light was lit once again, warning mariners of the Diamond Shoals and welcoming residents and visitors once again to the shores of Hatteras Island.

With the lighthouse mated to its new foundation, the contractors completed the installation of the two keepers' quarters and the oil house, bringing the Cape Hatteras Light Station back to its original configuration 2,900 feet from where Simpson and Stetson had built it in 1870—and 1,600 feet from the sea.

CHAPTER VI

THE BEACON STANDS

In the flames of opposition,
the merits of an idea
Are tempered or consumed.
Only in the doing is the proof.
What was begun is completed
And for this watch the danger passed.
—Mike Booher, December 1999

During the year following the relocation of Cape Hatteras Light Station, the National Park Service began the second of three phases of work that will enable the Park to better serve visitors and protect this unique cultural resource. Visitors started climbing the lighthouse again in May 2000, and surveyors returned periodically to check for any measurable movement or tilt of the lighthouse on its new foundation. Hatteras Light was found to be standing tall and steady.[1]

JHC Construction was awarded the phase two contract and started infrastructure enhancements at the station in October 1999. This $1.3 million package of work included an access road, parking facilities, comfort station, generator building, landscaping, and walkways so the Hatteras Lighthouse could be rededicated in the spring of 2001. Phase three plans included a dedicated visitors' center and museum shop, as well as a nearby beach facility. The double keepers' quarters, which has long served as an on-site museum, will continue to play that role at the new site, but the principal keeper's quarters, appropriately furnished, will be used to interpret the daily lives of the keepers of the light.

The famous lighthouse at its new home was lit again at a re-lighting ceremony November 13, 1999.

Phase two contractors worked in 2000 to prepare the light station for rededication, landscaping the site, laying walkways, opening a new restroom and providing parking for visitors.

Public Information Officer Bob Woody took many of the digital photographs that were used on the Park's web site, *www.nps.gov/caha/lrp.htm*, to keep the public informed.

While rededicating this coastal tower in 2001 to the memory of mariners, keepers, and a bygone way of life will generate interest among the press, regular visitors, and island residents, it is unlikely that the ceremony will put the lighthouse back into the same intense spotlight as did its relocation. Preserving a lighthouse that stands over 200 feet tall was not an ordinary preservation task. Moving it intact over half a mile down a sandy path was not an everyday move, even for an industry that specializes in relocating structures with unusual demands. And Cape Hatteras Light is a highly recognizable American icon. Its move was controversial and expensive. These were ingredients that guaranteed media coverage. Local and regional media representatives followed the story closely for years, but when the preparations for the move started in late 1998 and early 1999 the interest expanded. While the tower crept down the beach, international media broadcast the story worldwide.

But Bob Woody, the Park Service's Public Information Officer at the Outer Banks Group, believed that the public deserved even more of the story than they would read in the newspaper or see on the evening news. He used the Internet to provide a constant window through which "visitors" could access the work site.[2] Woody updated the web pages daily, posting progress photographs and marking important milestones. Public tax dollars were making this project possible, and the public watched as their money was spent. A web camera, sponsored by CBS affiliate WITN, captured live action from the top of the lighthouse, looking down and "ahead." The image was refreshed every two minutes for the hundreds of thousands of Internet users that followed the move from their desks. Tom Skinner of WITN said that "more stories about the lighthouse move went out on satellite from WITN to NBC affiliates than any other story in the history of the station and more people visited the lighthouse via their web site than attended Disney World that year."[3] It was a popular story.

Capitol Broadcasting, owner of five television stations in North Carolina, also helped capture the dynamic action of the move. This communications company sent a steady stream of photographers from WRAL-TV to film the relocation. In the two documentaries that Capitol Broadcasting produced using this exclusive footage, the filmmakers told many of the personal stories associated with this big engineering feat.

Capitol Broadcasting donated several thousand hours of film to the Park Service for its archives.

The media is known for its use of hyperbole to capture attention. Engineers are not. But both communities labeled the relocation of the Cape Hatteras Lighthouse the "move of the century." The American Society of Civil Engineers presented the National Park Service with its Outstanding Civil Engineering Achievement Award in 2000 and designated the lighthouse as a National Civil Engineering Historic Landmark. Law Engineering and Environmental Services, one of the major subcontractors for the relocation, accepted four awards for the project. The Consulting Engineers Council of North Carolina awarded the company its Grand Award for Engineering Excellence in Special Projects for Law's geotechnical study. The American Consulting Engineers Council provided Law its Grand Award for Excellence in Engineering Design. A Grand Award for Engineering Excellence came from the Metro Atlanta Engineering Week Committee. And the Association of Conservation Engineers presented Law its 2000 Award of Honor. International Chimney and Expert House Movers received accolades from the International Association of Structural Movers, including its Millennium Award, for this landmark move of an historic structure so tall and heavy, a move many of the

Thousands of visitors flocked to the move site during the spring and summer of 1999 to watch firsthand as the lighthouse was prepared and as it journeyed down the beach. A dedicated team of nearly 50 volunteers served as interpreters, stationed along the corridor. Visitors didn't seem to mind the makeshift paths through the woods, the insects, or the heat. They wanted to see the move for themselves and would wait for hours for the next "push." The volunteers patiently explained how it was being done and, more importantly, why. One group of volunteers posed in front of the principal keeper's quarters in March 1999 with Rany Jennette, seated front row, the son of the last Cape Hatteras Lighthouse principal keeper, Unaka Jennette. *See Appendix B for a list of those volunteers who are known to have assisted the Park Service during the relocation.*

Association's members took part in at the invitation of the Matyiko brothers.

Along with the awards came personal reflections. In a special edition of the *Island Breeze*, a monthly publication popular on the Outer Banks, Daniel C. Couch of Buxton shared the results of his conversations about Cape Hatteras Lighthouse with long-time island residents. He wrote:

> Hatteras Islanders cherish their memories of the Cape Hatteras Lighthouse, a monument that has become part of the fabric of their daily lives. For many generations, the grand old beacon has stood as a stalwart symbol of a way of life of people who pride themselves on a unique history and heritage.

The men and women Couch talked to spoke of courting by the Light, baseball games, Easter egg hunts, fishing and swimming, and dramatic rescues. Beatrice Barnett McArthur of Buxton grew up on stories of the U.S. Lifesaving Service, her father having been a part of this important rescue crew. Of the lighthouse move, she remarked:

> I feel like all those memories are being thrown away. I'm going to miss the lighthouse where it was. Some people have said we were apathetic about the move. The islanders were like the "mouse that roared"—it was a done deal and a day late before we ever made our feelings known about the move.

Barbara Barnett Williams, whose family included members of the Lighthouse and Lifesaving Services and the U.S. Coast Guard, told Couch that "History and heritage on Hatteras Island contribute greatly to its appeal." She wasn't sure if the relocation would have an impact on people's perception of history, but she went on to remark:

> I know the promotion end of it will be different—the sea and beach is out of the picture now. Somehow, to me, it's not going to be the same. Those days and memories are going right on down the beach, gone with the lighthouse. We'll have to wait and see.[4]

In the same edition of the *Island Breeze*, resident Irene Nolan echoed those sentiments. She wrote of the old site where Hatteras Light had stood for almost 130 years: "It all seems such a very undignified ending for a place that has been so much for so many." She revealed that she and many of her neighbors thought that the lighthouse should not have been moved; being "claimed by the sea would have been a fitting end for the beloved landmark." But as a journalist, she covered the story in detail and became a part of the regular media corps who attended frequent press briefings and often visited the site. She came to know the men and women behind the move. Of the day the lighthouse landed at its new location she wrote:

> I forgot my notions about the move away from the sea and was exhilarated by that moment of triumph of the human mind and spirit. . . . It was, as so many have said, "the move of the century." It was a once-in-a-lifetime experience. It was an incredible engineering feat that was pulled off by men whose passion for the lighthouse equals that of many islanders.[5]

Dedication, trust and teamwork were very important to this engineering accomplishment, according to International Chimney's Joe Jakubik. At his first internal team meeting, he had told his partners that they were part of this team because "they were the best at what they did." He believed that the team members "developed an extraordinary level of trust in each other." Jakubik had stressed that decisions concerning resources and manpower were to be made on the "basis of what was best for the project and not necessarily what was best for an individual team member, including International Chimney Corporation." It all came down to a matter of pride in making a contribution to preserving this important historic structure. "No one wanted to be the one to let the rest of the team and project down. Sometimes, it's as simple as that," Jakubik said.[6] As team leader, project manager Jakubik juggled concerns over safety, schedule, historic integrity, and budget at two lighthouse sites that summer. ICC was also restoring the Tybee Island Lighthouse near Savannah, Georgia. Jakubik's specailty was overseeing ICC's historic property work, and he traveled between the two sites.

Bill Harris, former Superintendent of Cape Hatteras National Seashore, is also a life-long resident of the Outer Banks. The idea of saving the lighthouse by surrounding it with a revetment was a serious option on his watch, and he had believed at the time that it had merit. But the people who moved the Hatteras Lighthouse, once the decision was made to do so, did a wonderful job, he said, and he had visited the site many times to watch the progress. With all the care given to preserving the relationships of the buildings to one another and to the sea, however, Harris wondered why the plan had not also included the preservation of the historic view shed. The lighthouse is in the woods now, and it hadn't looked like that when either Dearborn or Stetson had built their towers, he mused. But time will give us back the view—and the problem.[7]

On Memorial Day 2000, the Park Service officially re-opened the Cape Hatteras Lighthouse to visitors.

The North Carolina Geodetic Survey installed four special commemorative survey disks, designed by John David Hardee, onto the Cape Hatteras Lighthouse. One 4-inch brass disk was installed on the catwalk and three on the base. Survey disks mark positions on the Earth's surface with known geographic locations and are utilized by surveyors. The new markers replaced the original survey benchmarks (below) installed by the U.S. Coast and Geodetic Survey.

"I've never worked on a project that was as technically challenging and as important to so many people as the move of the lighthouse," said National Park Service's Dan McClarren. In the process of overseeing operations on site every day, McClarren and the contractor team sometimes differed on the details, but International Chimney and Expert House Movers performed high-quality work under adverse conditions, he said. "And we moved the lighthouse while the world watched and while a lot of people were telling us it couldn't be done. It felt good to prove them wrong." Like most of the team, McClarren thrived on the excitement, the exposure, and the enormous challenge of moving and saving a structure that looked impossible to move. A job this important would come his way only once, and he was grateful for having had the opportunity to contribute.[8]

For Bob Woody of the National Park Service, the relocation was about saving history and providing environmental leadership. Saving the lighthouse with a revetment would have sent the wrong signal. "Use groins or revetments and the statement was loud and clear that development would dominate," he said. But relocating the lighthouse "would demonstrate that natural coastal processes and the environment it produces is not only important, but also critical to the health of our coastal lands." Woody, in his 33 years with the Park Service, had never worked with "a group of people who were so committed, so focused, on a task as were the men and women of International Chimney Corporation and their subcontractors, the Volunteers-In-The-Park, and the employees of Cape Hatteras National Seashore." He remarked that being a part of something this important and historic would only happen to him once, and he was privileged to have had a hand in its accomplishment. But more important than personal pride of the moment was the lasting contribution this team made:

Saving the lighthouse was about passing along to future generations those symbols that embody values representative of the best of the American character. The Cape Hatteras Lighthouse is a vessel of the American experience, a symbol of the lightkeepers and their families and the way they lived their lives—with dedication, courage, commitment, care and concern for their responsibilities and for the people who made their livelihood from the sea. In the spirit of those lightkeepers past, our generation stepped up to the challenge to see that tangible evidence of those values was passed on to future generations.

The men and women of the Cape Hatteras Lighthouse relocation team did more than move a lighthouse. They saved a symbol of American maritime history and an icon that represents coastal life. To truly understand history, we must walk where others walked. For another 100 years or more, visitors should be able to follow the steps of the builders and keepers of the Cape Hatteras Lighthouse, even though those 257 step-worn stairs are now 2,900 feet further down the sandy beach of Hatteras Island.

◆

PHOTOGRAPHER'S SCRAPBOOK

With the completion of this book and the rededication of the Cape Hatteras Light Station in the spring of 2001 comes closure for me. I have but one regret. There are so many individuals to whom I am indebted who made this experience possible. No publication may ever satisfy my need to say thank you, but I hope you will enjoy these few additional "people shots" from my project scrapbook. *Mike Booher*

Rick Lohr

Jerry Stockbridge

Willard Gray

Dave Fischetti

Partners Progress Meeting

Attitude

Jones, Olin, and Austin

Randy Knott

Richie Meekins

Expert Housemovers of Virginia

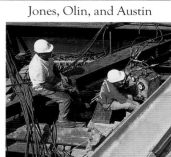
Jim and Sara Matyiko

Olin, Riker, and Hunt

Joe Mason

Joe Jakubik

Rollinson, Wescott, Blackmon

Steve Crum

John Mayne

Steve Ryan

John Matyiko III

APPENDIX A
CHRONOLGY OF EVENTS 1773-1998

1773 Alexander Hamilton, aboard the *Thunderbolt*, experienced the fury of the seas near the Diamond Shoals during a north-bound journey to Boston.

1784 North Carolina selected Smith Island (later named Bald Head Island) in the mouth of the Cape Fear River as the site for the state's first lighthouse.

1789 North Carolina passed legislation to build a lighthouse on Ocracoke Island.

At Hamilton's urging, Congress passed the Lighthouse Bill, which included a directive to investigate the feasibility of constructing a lighthouse at Cape Hatteras. The new U.S. Treasury Department's Revenue Cutter Service assumed responsibility for constructing, maintaining, and repairing all light stations.

1792 Congress appropriated $4,000 to complete Bald Head (Smith Island) Light.

1794 Congress authorized a lighthouse to be built at Cape Hatteras, and Tenche Cox, first Commissioner of Revenue, began the task of purchasing land on Hatteras Island upon which to build it.

Congress approved Old Rock (later named Shell Castle Island) as the location for a lighthouse to mark Ocracoke Inlet.

Cox solicited bids for the construction of both Outer Banks lights.

1795 Smith Island Light became operational; supplementaty appropriations brought the total construction cost to $12,000.

1798 William Miller, second Commissioner of Revenue, accepted the revised bid of Henry Dearborn to construct the Hatteras and Ocracoke light stations for $38,450 and released $8,000 to purchase materials for Hatteras.

1799 Work began at the Hatteras site in September.

1800 The North Carolina General Assembly ratified legislation completing the transfer of four acres on Hatteras Island to the Treasury Department for the construction of a lighthouse, which had already commenced.

The 55-foot-tall wooden Ocracoke Inlet Light was lit.

1801 Total cost of Hatteras Light projected at $39,000.

1802 Dearborn completed the octagonal sandstone Hatteras Lighthouse. It stood 112 feet above the sea.

1803 With Adam Gaskins serving as the first Hatteras keeper, the Hatteras Lighthouse became operational.

1804 1,000-gallon cisterns for storing whale oil to fuel the Hatteras lamps were replaced with 2,000-gallon cisterns.

1806 A fall storm damaged Hatteras Light and forced it out of service for over a month.

1809 A fire, sparked by an oil spill in the Hatteras lantern room, destroyed the glass of that room in January.

A wire enclosure was installed around the lantern room's exterior to protect the glass from birds that flew into it.

1810 Sand eroded from the base of Hatteras Light, exposing 4 feet of its foundation.

1812 Hatteras Light's lantern system was replaced by new lamps and parabolic reflectors designed by Winslow Lewis.

1813 Because Hatteras Light was damaged by the British during the War of 1812, it was closed in September of that year. Samuel Wilkins repaired the light, and it was put back in service.

1817 Better quality oil was substituted for that originally specified for the Hatteras lanterns, in response to complaints that the light was dim and at times unlit.

1823 Augustin Fresnel invented a new lens system for lighthouses that used prisms and magnifying lenses to focus the beam. This improved system was adopted throughout Europe.

1824 A lightship was anchored at the outer edge of the Diamond Shoals to supplement Hatteras Light.

1827 The Diamond Shoals lightship was destroyed during a storm in the vicinity of Ocracoke Inlet.

New keepers' quarters constructed at Hatteras Station.

1828 The Government purchased 40 more acres, increasing the size of the Cape Hatteras Light Station.

1835 Hatteras Light was outfitted with new lantern reflectors.

1845 Hatteras Light's 14-inch reflectors were replaced with 15-inch reflectors, but complaints about visibility continued.

1848 A new lantern system—15 reflectors, each with a 21-inch diameter—was installed in the Hatteras lantern room.

The Revenue Cutter Service established a coastal life-saving service at Cape Hatteras

1850 In response to increased sand erosion from Hatteras Light, a fence was built at its base.

1852 Hatteras Light was supplemented by a floating bell beacon at Diamond Shoals, which survived four months.

Beacon Island Light, 39 feet high, was built near Ocracoke Inlet.

At the request of Congress, Treasury directed a panel of experts to investigate the efficacy of the U.S. lighthouse system. The experts declared the system inadequate and under-funded, inspiring Congress to create a Lighthouse Board to supervise the network of lighthouses.

1853 A light vessel was stationed in the vicinity of Ocracoke Inlet.

1854 The Lighthouse Board allocated $15,000 to increase the height of the Hatteras Lighthouse to 150 feet, install a first-order Fresnel lens system, paint the Lighthouse to improve its daytime visibility (whitewashed from base to 70 feet; red above that), and construct new keepers' quarters.

1856 A 25-foot-high beacon was erected to mark the entrance to Pamlico Sound on the southern end of Hatteras Island.

1859 The 150-foot-high Cape Lookout Lighthouse was built 40 miles south of Hatteras.

1861 During the Civil War, Confederate soldiers removed the lens from Hatteras Light, extinguishing it, but they were unable to carry out their plans to destroy the structure when Union forces occupied the island.

1862 Hatteras Light was restored with a less powerful lens and put back in operation.

The USS Monitor sunk while under tow south of Cape Hatteras; 16 men drowned.

1863 A first-order Fresnel lens was once again installed at Hatteras.

1867 Brigatine George Malthy and schooner Vesta were lost off Cape Hatteras. These highly publicized losses prompted vessel owners to complain that lighthouse improvements were still needed to warn captains of the dangerous Diamond Shoals. Congress approved $75,000 for construction of a new Cape Hatteras Lighthouse 600 feet north of the first, 1,500 feet from the sea. The new structure was designed by Lighthouse Board engineers.

1868 The Lighthouse Board hired Dexter Stetson as foreman of the Hatteras construction crew and Benjamin Jennett as principal keeper.

1869 Stetson supervised the building of an overland transportation system for materials that would be delivered to Hatteras Island on the sound side, shelters for the crew, a blacksmith shop, storehouses, derricks, and the octagonal base, tower, and lantern room of the lighthouse itself.

1870 Construction of the 208-foot-high new Cape Hatteras Light was completed and the kerosene fuel lantern lit. Construction cost $155,000.

Congress approved funding for additional lighthouses to be built in North Carolina and for seven life-saving stations that would be part of the reorganized Life-Saving Service overseen by the Treasury Department.

1871 Principal keeper's quarters were built near Hatteras Light. The degraded old tower was destroyed by demolition.

1872 Bodie Island Light was completed, approximately 40 miles north of Hatteras Station.

1873 A paint scheme was approved for the North Carolina lighthouses, which included unique twisting alternating black and white stripes for Hatteras.

1874 The entrance to Pamlico Sound was marked by a small screw-pile light on the southern end of Hatteras Island.

1875 Currituck Beach, the fourth "coastal tower" lighthouse, was completed.

1879 Lightning struck Hatteras Light, and without proper grounding, the brickwork cracked. A large metal plate was buried in the sand to ensure proper grounding, and the brickwork damage was repaired.

1884 A whistling buoy was installed at the Diamond Shoals to supplement the Hatteras Light, but it failed.

1888 The U.S. Army Corps of Engineers published a plan for building an off-shore lit tower on the Diamond Shoals at an estimated cost of $300,000 to $500,000.

1890 The Lighthouse Board opened bids for the construction of a Diamond Shoals tower.

1891 Construction began on the Diamond Shoals tower, but early work was destroyed by currents and storm conditions. The project was cancelled and the remaining funds earmarked for the construction of a new lightship.

1894 The Lighthouse Board considered a second design for a Diamond Shoals tower but did not act on it.

1897 A new Diamond Shoals lightship (LV 69) went to sea to supplement the lighthouse's beacon.

1899 LV 69 was washed ashore during a hurricane, repaired, and sent back to the Diamond Shoals.

1901 LV 69 retired from duty on Diamond Shoals and was replaced by LV 71 and 72, alternating sea duty off Hatteras Island.

1904 The Lighthouse Board approved another design for a Diamond Shoals tower, but it was not built because the financial risk to the private investor was too great.

1912 An incandescent oil vapor lamp was installed in the Hatteras lantern room, significantly increasing the intensity of the light.

1915 The Revenue Cutter Service and the Life-Saving Service combined to become the U.S. Coast Guard.

1918 A World War I German submarine fired on the anchored LV 71 after its crew sent warnings of the sub's position to other vessels. The crew was allowed to leave ship before being sunk by the submarine.

1919 Observers noted that the base of the Hatteras Lighthouse was now approximately 300 feet from the ocean. Local efforts to restore shrubs and grasses helped stabilize the sandy soil; the first artificial dunes were constructed.

1930s Bridges and paved roads brought development to the Nags Head area of the northern Outer Banks. The inconvenience of ferry service at Oregon and Ocracoke Inlets tempered growth on the southern islands.

Civilian Conservation Corps workers joined local residents in planting grasses, shrubs, and trees along the beaches of the Outer Banks. Additionally, they erected wind fences to hold blowing sand, thereby establishing a system of dunes. Sand was also pumped from one area to another to fill gaps in the beaches.

1933 Local interests expressed a desire to declare Hatteras Island a national seashore, protecting it from development.

1934 Electric generators were installed at the Hatteras Light Station, and the oil-burning lamp was replaced by an electric bulb.

1935 Landowners donated 999 acres in proximity to Cape Hatteras Light Station to North Carolina for a seashore park.

The state made it illegal to free-range livestock, which grazed on the vegetation that could help stabilize beaches. The National Park Service began contributing to the efforts to stabilize the beaches on Hatteras Island.

1936 Ocean water reached the Hatteras Lighthouse, and it was taken out of service. The light was extinguished.

A substitute skeleton steel tower with a beacon was constructed in nearby Buxton Woods.

1937 In response to the National Park Service's formal recommendation, Congress established the Cape Hatteras National Seashore to preserve the area as a "primitive wilderness," except for the eight existing villages already established on the islands (50 Stat. 669). Land acquisition for the new park, however, was limited to donations; while the Park Service waited for such donations, it became caretaker of some federal properties in the vicinity, including Hatteras Lighthouse. The Park Service renovated the double keepers' quarters and repainted the lighthouse.

1939 President Roosevelt ordered that the Lighthouse Service be merged with the U.S. Coast Guard. The Coast Guard assumed all responsibilities for lighthouse operations.

North Carolina established the Cape Hatteras Seashore Commission to assist the Park Service in obtaining land. The Commission suspended its work during the War years and began again in 1950.

1940 Authorizing legislation establishing the Cape Hatteras National Seashore was amended.

1942-45 Cape Hatteras Lighthouse served as a lookout tower to scan the ocean for World War II German submarines.

1946 The last Diamond Shoals lightship, WLV 189, entered service.

Congress extended the deadline for procuring land for the Cape Hatteras National Seashore to 1952.

1948 The ocean was 1,000 feet from Hatteras Lighthouse. The Park Service leased the structure back to the Coast Guard for active service and, together, the two agencies began repairing damage and preserving the tower.

1949 The interior and exterior of Hatteras Light were repainted, windows were replaced, and electrical service was installed to power an electric beacon with a 1,400-watt bulb.

1950 The Hatteras Lighthouse was put back in operation, and the steel tower's light was extinguished. An emergency generator was located in the old oil house. Operations were highly automated.

1953 With a private donation from the Paul Mellon family matched by State funding, the Park Service sought to purchase the remaining lands for the Cape Hatteras National Seashore. The Secretary of the Interior signed the order establishing the seashore recreation area.

1954 Hurricane Hazel caused significant damage to the Outer Banks.

1955 Hurricanes Connie, Diane, and Ione caused significant damage to the Outer Banks and prompted North Carolina to publish a hurricane report that served as a guide for coastal policy. The authors advocated beach stabilization and maintenance of sand dunes, along with stricter guidelines for coastal development and construction.

The U.S. Navy began operating a "listening post" just north of Cape Hatteras Lighthouse, fronting the beach.

1957 North Carolina passed legislation giving counties authority to require permits for dune and vegetation alterations.

1958 Cape Hatteras National Seashore was formally dedicated, and North Carolina formally deeded lands to the Federal Government for the new park unit.

1963 A bridge was built over Oregon Inlet, opening Hatteras Island to increased tourist visitation.

1965 North Carolina amended the Dune Protection Act of 1957, limiting local authority to those areas shoreward of previously established shore protection lines.

1966 312,000 cubic yards of sand were pumped onto the beach in front of Hatteras Light; the fine sand from the sound-side quickly washed away.

1967 An off-shore platform-style light station, built for the Coast Guard, replaced the last Diamond Shoals lightship.

The Park Service fortified the beach in front of Hatteras Light with sandbags.

At the Navy's request, the U.S. Army Corps of Engineers Coastal Engineering Research Center studied the shore erosion problem threatening its Hatteras Island installation just north of the lighthouse. The experts offered four alternatives and recommended the installation of a three-groin system, based on cost.

The Navy installed a nylon bag revetment along 1,100 feet of shoreline fronting its Hatteras Island installation; it deteriorated in three years.

1969 The Navy installed three reinforced concrete groins just north of Hatteras Light.

1971 The Park Service again added sand (200,000 cubic yards) to the beach near Hatteras Light, using material from the ocean side.

Dare County, in which Hatteras Island is located, finally adopted a local dune protection ordinance in reaction to a deadline mandated by the State.

The U.S. Army Corps of Engineers inventoried the condition of the U.S. shoreline, finding that 29 miles of the Cape Hatteras National Seashore shoreline needed some form of protection.

1972 A double beacon was installed in the Hatteras Light lantern room, each with a 1,000-watt bulb.

1973 The Park Service added more than one million cubic yards of sand to the Hatteras beachfront.

1974 The Park Service's Denver Service Center prepared a shoreline erosion policy statement, which described the features of the Cape Hatteras National Seashore, threats to the stability of the Park, and recommendations for actions in response to those threats. Five alternatives for action ranged from letting nature take its course with no interference to taking aggressive stabilization action to protect threatened areas, such as the lighthouse. This report also suggested studying the feasibility of relocating threatened historic structures, including Hatteras Light.

Duke University coastal geologist Orrin H. Pilkey advocated that the Park Service study's first alternative, no human interference, was most ideal, but that the second alternative was more politically feasible: a combination of not impeding natural processes, prohibiting structural control measures, maintaining ground transportation links, working with the Corps of Engineers, and studying alternatives to protect the historic Hatteras Lighthouse.

1975 The Navy reinforced the damaged groins they had installed in 1969. The ocean was 600 feet from Hatteras Light.

The North Carolina Department of Natural and Economic Resources studied the 1974 Park Service shoreline erosion policy and endorsed a modified alternative two.

Local residents, in response to the 1974 report, advocated a series of short-term solutions, what the report's authors described as the "no new action" alternative: continue dune building and stabilization efforts, do not impede further development, adopt extensive stabilization measures to save the Cape Hatteras Lighthouse, or move it if it cannot be saved in place.

The Superintendent of the Seashore and the Southeast Regional Director called for the preparation of an environmental statement, along with an environmental management policy that responds to the natural processes of the island environment rather than attempting to artificially control a changeable landscape.

1976 The Park Service continued work on its description of the Cape Hatteras environment and a preferred alternative (a modified version of alternative two presented in the 1974 study) for its seashore management policy.

1977 The Park Service directed the Denver Service Center to prepare an environmental assessment of the Cape Hatteras National Seashore.

The Coast Guard automated the light of Diamond Shoals tower.

1978 In a status report, National Park Service managers at the Seashore described their work on a management strategy: no stabilization of the shoreline; maintenance of transportation links in the event of inlet changes; no interference with the dune system, except where human activity threatens it.

1979 Engineer David C. Fischetti provided consultation services to the Park Service as part of their feasibility study to relocate Cape Hatteras Light.

1980 A storm eradicated the last remnants of the foundation of the original Hatteras Lighthouse. Two strong storms helped decrease the width of the beach that separated Hatteras Light from the ocean from 150 feet to 70 feet. Temporary protective sheet pile groins were erected east and south of the lighthouse, and sandbags were added to the beachfront.

The Park Service contracted with MTMA Design Group to study protection alternatives for the Cape Hatteras Lighthouse. The authors' six alternatives ranged from taking no action, to moving it, to stabilizing and protecting it by a variety of means.

Local residents formed the Outer Banks Preservation Association to prevent the loss of the lighthouse.

A National Aeronautics and Space Administration engineer at the Kennedy Space Center was asked by the Superintendent of Cape Canaveral National Seashore to comment on the feasibility of relocating the Hatteras Lighthouse. The engineer, in his informal communication, believed that there were risks and that the costs projected were too low.

1981 Businessman Hugh Morton established the Save the Cape Hatteras Lighthouse Committee, co-chaired by Governor of North Carolina James Hunt and U.S. Senator Jesse Helms. The Committee's goal was to raise $1 million to preserve the structure.

109

The National Park Service released its Cape Hatteras National Seashore environmental assessment, general management plan, and development concept plan for public comment.

An artificial seaweed product made of polypropylene was installed to assist with erosion prevention near the Hatteras Light.

The National Park Service requested the Corps of Engineers to develop a long-term plan for protecting Cape Hatteras Light. The Corps offered two alternatives: 4 inshore breakwaters and a terminal groin; or a secured seawall. Additionally, the Park Service asked the Corps to devise an interim protection plan and to prepare a scope of work whereby the feasibility of relocating the lighthouse could be ascertained.

1982 Lee Wan & Associates estimated the cost of segmental relocation and reconstruction of the Hatteras Light 3,000 feet inland at $5.5 million.

Fischetti submitted documents in response to a request from the Corps of Engineers, Wilmington District, to perform an engineering analysis of the Cape Hatteras Lighthouse as part of the decision-making process to determine the best method to protect the structure.

Public opinion to alternatives proposed by the National Park Service to save Cape Hatteras Light favored the construction of a protective revetment, or seawall, around it. As the shoreline moved west, the lighthouse would be left in the surf as an island. The Park Service agreed to fund this alternative, estimated at $6 million. The Corps ceased its work on preparing a scope of work to determine the feasibility of moving the lighthouse.

700 more sandbags were added to the beach, and additional artificial seaweed product, paid for by the Save Cape Hatteras Lighthouse Committee, was "planted" to assist with erosion prevention near the Hatteras Light.

1983 In "Coastal Erosion at Cape Hatteras: A Lighthouse in Danger," University of Virginia scientists Lorance Dix Lisle and Robert Dolan predicted that without a major engineering effort to save it, the lighthouse would probably be destroyed within 10 years during a major coastal storm.

Fischetti informed Morton of the Save the Lighthouse Committee of his firm's desire to provide an engineering analysis of the Hatteras Lighthouse to determine if it could be safely moved.

The Corps of Engineers installed a scour protection apron for the remaining groin near the Hatteras Lighthouse as part of the interim protection plan designed by the Corps at the request of the Park Service.

1984 The Park Service issued an amended environmental assessment and an updated general management plan for the Cape Hatteras National Seashore for review. Actions proposed included: controlling off-road vehicles, allowing natural seashore dynamics to occur unless the transportation link or other significant resources are threatened, controlling exotic species, preparing studies and action plans to ensure that natural and cultural resources are preserved, and cooperating with state and local governments to realize mutually beneficial planning objectives. The authors did not consider protection options for the lighthouse in this plan.

The North Carolina Department of Natural Resources and Community Development's Coastal Resources Commission's Outer Banks Erosion Task Force submitted a report. In it, the experts noted the Park Service's decision to design a revetment to protect the Hatteras Light; the report went on to state that seawalls and revetments do not protect beachfront and do increase erosion.

1985 The North Carolina Department of Coastal Management stated that it would require the Park Service to apply for a variance to its prohibition against the use of hardened structures, such as the revetment proposed around Hatteras Light.

Hasbrouck-Hunderman Architects were awarded a contract to conduct a comprehensive structural analysis of Cape Hatteras Lighthouse at a cost of $138,207.

The Corps of Engineers' Wilmington District submitted its design for a seawall and revetment for Hatteras Light.

1986 A Corps of Engineers inspection revealed that the scour apron installed at the southern groin in 1983 had suffered damage.

Hasbrouck Hunderman, with Wiss, Janney, Elstner Associates, submitted a comprehensive structural analysis of the Hatteras Lighthouse and a preservation program report that detailed necessary repairs that should be made. The North Carolina Historic Preservation Officer concurred with the plan.

Fischetti, President of the Move the Lighthouse Committee, recommended to the Director of the National Park Service that the agency reevaluate its decision to surround the Hatteras Light with a revetment and reconsider relocating it instead.

1987 The National Park Service requested the National Academy of Sciences' National Research Council to conduct a 90-day study of the two leading options for protecting the Cape Hatteras Lighthouse: relocating it or surrounding it with a revetment. The academic body agreed to conduct the study, but over a nine month period, for an estimated cost of $75,000. The interim report submitted to the Park Service favored relocation.

A campaign of letter-writing and editorials favoring relocation over the revetment option was conducted, with letters coming from structural engineers, professional movers, geologists, and other professionals. The Hatteras Island Business Association and other local groups remained opposed to moving it, however.

National Park Service Director William Penn Mott, Jr., asked the Southeast Regional Director to review the decision-making process that led the Park Service to favor the revetment option.

Solicitation of bids to construct the revetment was tabled.

1988 The National Academy of Sciences in its final report recommended that the Cape Hatteras Lighthouse be moved in increments. The first move, 400-600 feet to the southwest, would protect it for 25 years. The report suggested that it would take one year to prepare for the three-month relocation effort. Cost to move the lighthouse 500 feet was estimated at $4.6 million.

The National Park Service Denver Service Center prepared an estimate of costs associated with overseeing the design and construction contract process in support of relocating Hatteras Light. The Center was also directed to assess each of the alternatives offered in the National Academy of Sciences report and offer a preferred solution, along with a development plan for that solution and an environmental assessment.

The Superintendent of Cape Hatteras National Seashore advocated a move site in the range of 2,000 feet rather than the incremental move recommended by the Academy. This would provide approximately 50 years of protection. Upon further reflection, the Park Service planned for a 2,500-foot move, designed to keep the beacon safe for 100 years, at a cost of $7 million. Park Service and Corps of Engineers staff marked the relocation site, and the Corps prepared to perform the necessary topographical survey and take test borings along the move corridor. The Park Service also began working with the Corps to plan for rehabilitating the existing groins to provide interim protection.

1989 Hasbrouck Peterson Associates, with Wiss, Janney, Elstner Associates, presented construction details for the proposed Hatteras Lighthouse preservation work.

The Park received notice that the relocation proposal had passed the mandated 106 compliance milestone, a process required to assess actions that would impact an historic structure.

The Park Service distributed the Hatteras Lighthouse relocation environmental assessment and protection alternatives document for comment and gave the Corps the notice to proceed with the prescribed site work. The Corps concluded that the move corridor was acceptable for that purpose.

110

At the end of the public comment period, the Cape Hatteras Superintendent summarized the reactions to the lighthouse protection alternatives document: elected officials and residents opposed relocation, and Congressional support was not in place for funding it. He proposed postponing the relocation until the risk to the lighthouse was greater. The Southeast Regional Director concurred, hoping that the intervening time could be used to educate the public about the relocation.

1990 More sandbagging—and supplemental funding to provide for it—was required in the vicinity of the Hatteras Lighthouse. The Park Service sought funding for its interim protection plan and approval for the relocation at a future date. The Denver Service Center was instructed to continue with the environmental compliance work required for the move, and a draft finding of no significant impact on the environment was signed.

1991 The Park Service announced the design competition for the lighthouse relocation project and began evaluating bids. The project, however, was tabled.

1992 Again, the Denver Service Center was directed to oversee design and construction services for the Cape Hatteras Lighthouse move.

The Save the Lighthouse Committee donated nearly $11,000 to repair the lighthouse roof.

The Park Service established a committee of experts led by Robert Dolan to further evaluate the interim protection plan designed in 1988 but not carried out. The committee recommended proceeding with the move of the lighthouse by fall 1994. Meanwhile, the Park Service reprogrammed over $3 million originally designated for the Hatteras project to conduct repairs at other seashore parks, leaving $777,000 for emergency stabilization efforts.

International Chimney Corporation, under contract, repaired and restored Cape Hatteras Lighthouse.

1993 The National Park Service asked the Corps of Engineers to design an enhanced sandbag buffer system and to engineer interim protection measures. The interim measures again included a fourth groin, which was to be designed by 1995.

1994 The Park Service prepared the necessary documents for public comment on the rehabilitation of the south groin and notified the public about the proposed fourth groin.

Hurricane Gordon damage required the addition of 380 more sandbags to the beach in front of Hatteras Light.

1995 The U.S. Fish and Wildlife Service opposed the fourth groin proposal.

Damage from Hurricanes Felix and Luis required approximately 300 new sandbags for the beachfront at Hatteras Light.

1996 Dolan and his colleagues again called for the relocation of the lighthouse to proceed as soon as possible.

Public meetings were scheduled to review the fourth groin proposal, and the Corps delivered its design report. The 800-foot steel groin would be installed 650 feet south of the existing south groin. The North Carolina Department of Cultural Resources declared that it was time to relocate the lighthouse and opposed the fourth groin, as did the North Carolina Department of Coastal Management. Dolan reported that downdrift erosion caused by the fourth groin would adversely impact the lighthouse relocation site.

The North Carolina Department of Coastal Management approved a proposal to add another 300 sandbags to the Hatteras Light beach.

President pro tempore of the North Carolina Senate Marc Basnight requested that North Carolina State University provide a professional review of and update to the National Academy of Sciences study of the Hatteras Lighthouse situation.

1997 The North Carolina State University ad hoc panel declared that relocating the lighthouse was the only feasible option, that the structure would be destroyed if it were not moved, and that the move should be accomplished by spring 1999.

Cape Hatteras National Seashore managers concurred with the University report and set the target date for the move: May 1999. The Park authorized an archaeological survey team to begin its inspection of the new site and move corridor; no archaeological findings of significance were reported. The proposed move distance was increased to 2,900 feet; the cost was calculated at $12 million. Answering a request for qualifications, six potential contractors asked to be considered for the relocation project.

The Dare County Board of Commissioners opposed the relocation and advocated the installation of a fourth groin.

1998 After a panel evaluated the qualifications of potential contractors, the Park Service invited two of the six to respond to a request for proposals for the relocation design and relocation of Cape Hatteras Lighthouse. On June 19, the Park Service awarded the design-build contract to International Chimney, obligating fiscal year 1998 funds. In December, with fiscal year 1999 monies, procurement officers exercised the construction option.

Local elected officials and citizens vocally opposed plans to proceed with the move.

Law Engineering and Environmental Services submitted a geotechnical investigation report, which found the proposed new site and move corridor acceptable.

Wiss, Janney, Elstner Associates submitted a structural materials investigation report and a supplemental report discussing the timber mat upon which the Lighthouse's foundation was built.

International Chimney submitted its detailed relocation procedures plan, and construction mobilization began before the end of the year.

The Park was notified that 106 compliances impacting the structures of the Hatteras Light Station had been achieved.

The second phase of the construction project—visitor services, parking, and utility infrastructure—was assigned to Denver Service Center for design.

The Dare County Board of Commissioners filed a complaint and motion for a temporary restraining order, preliminary injunction, and permanent injunction in Federal Court to halt or delay the project. A Federal judge denied the Commissioners' motions.

APPENDIX B
THE LIGHTHOUSE MOVERS

It took hundreds of dedicated people to prepare for and move the Cape Hatteras Light Station. In addition to those shown in this book, many others labored behind the scenes. The following lists of personnel, volunteers, and friends of the project were provided by the participating organizations.

National Park Service
CAPE HATTERAS
NATIONAL SEASHORE

Bob Reynolds, *Superintendent*

Chris Bernthal, *Deputy Superintendent*

Dan McClarren, *Chief of Maintenance/Project Site Supervisor*

John Wescott, *South District Maintenance Foreman/Assistant Project Site Supervisor*

Bob Woody, *Public Information Officer/Information Liaison*

Rob Bolling, *Historian/Assistant Public Information Officer*

Steve Harrison, *Chief of Resource Management Division*

Jeff Cobb, *Chief of Resource and Visitor Protection Division*

Steve Ryan, *South District Ranger, Resource and Visitor Protection Division*

Dennis Atkins, *Engineer, Survey Team*

Charlie Snow, *Engineer, Survey Team*

National Park Service
DENVER SERVICE CENTER

David Laux, *Project Manager, through May 1999*

Paul Cloyd, *Contracting Officer's Representative, 1997-June 1999; Project Manager, May 1999-completion*

Judy Hauser, *Contracting Officer, 1997-April 1999*

Steve Eckelberg, *Contracting Officer, April 1999-October 1999*

Ellen Sanders, *Contracting Specialist, 1997-January 1999*

Marlene Haussler, *Contracting Specialist, June-September 1999*

CITIZENS
EXCEPTIONAL SERVICE

Bert Austin, Sheriff, Dare County

Senator Marc Basnight, North Carolina Senate

Dr. Ellis Cowling, North Carolina State University

Governor James Hunt, North Carolina

Lt. Cmdr. Christopher Olin, United States Coast Guard

Dr. Paul Zia, North Carolina State University

CONGRESSIONAL
EXCEPTIONAL SERVICE

Lauch Faircloth, *U.S. Senator, North Carolina*

PARK VOLUNTEERS

Michelle Adcock
Bonnie Baker
Mary Basnight
Mike Booher
Ben & Thea Bova
Don & Sharon Brown
Cay Carich
Howard & Elaine Cator
John & Brenda Coffey
Jinx Caylor
Audrey Conner
Vicky Cox
Nancy D'Andrade
Mary Dickens
Hester Fink
Needra Ford
Bob Gaul
Nancy Giannotti
Larry & Dee Hardham
Connie Hartung
Lynn & Windsor Jacques
Lynn Jennette
Sveta Krestinina
Ken Lapeyre
Frank & Gloria Marshall
Wayne Mathis
Bob & Betty May
Richard Meissner
Howard & Jean Meyer
John Newdorp
Sara Officer
Suzanne Quinlan
Dave & Doris Reed

Ivar Rundgren
Richard Schneider
Harold Shafer
Jean Simmons
Whit Summers
Buck Tauben
Victor Vernon III
Joan Vail
Charlie & Shirley Votaw
Frances Westerfield
Katya Zorina

INTERNATIONAL CHIMNEY
CORPORATION

Terry Barksdale
Timothy Crimmins
Shane Cullen
John Devine
Oswald Edwards
Jefferey Fellows
Raymond Fisher
Jim Flemming
Christopher Ford
Joseph Fortin
George Gardner
Ed Gasiecki
David Gates
Willard Gray
Erin Green
Ed Guindon
Robert Hayes III
Kim Haynes
Thomas Heggie
Robert Henning
Stephen Hesseler
Larry Horch
Skellie Hunt
Joe Jakubik
Rick Lohr, *President*
Richard Mailhot
James Markley
Michael Martin
Christopher Matney
Daniel May
Richard Meekins
John Mitchell
Milburn Pack
Marvin Patrick
David Pawson
Robert Penfield
Carroll Price
Benjamin Quidley
Maurice Quidley

Michael Riddick
Luis Rodriguez
William Saunders
Alan Scarborough
Clyde Scarborough
Gary Schulz
Steven Scyoc
Robert Simmons
Rick Speich
Christopher Thigpen
Michael Vacanti
Richard Vernon

EXPERT HOUSE MOVERS

Family Employees:
Frank Matyiko
Gabriel Matyiko
Geri Ellen Matyiko
Hance Matyiko
Jenna Matyiko
Jerry Matyiko, *President*
Jim Matyiko
Joan Mayiko
Joe Matyiko
Joe Matyiko, Jr.
John Matyiko, Jr.
John Matyiko III
John P. Matyiko
Sara Matyiko
Scott Matyiko
Travis Matyiko
Carrie & Jay Searles
Diane & Brian Searles
Pat & J. C. Taylor
Other Employees—
Arthur Baxter
Edward Baxter
Lonny Baxter
Kenny Bell
H. T. Bowes & Son
Vincent Carter
Shane Darnell
Lambert & Barbara Donaway
Robert Emans
James Ivey
Joseph Jones
Mike Landen
Jerry Laneer
Kevin Lucas
Sean McLaughlin
Joe Mason
Barry Mullins
Marvin Patrick
Vincent Pruitt

Keith Roberts
Herman Sanderson
Kelly Sanderson
Ivory Sanderson
W. D. Sanderson
Robert Winder
Peter Freisen, *Consultant*
Movers:
Kim Brownie
Chad Jonasson
Jerry Jonasson
Phil Jonasson
Jim Kabrick
Jeff Kennedy
J. C. Muehlfelt & Sons., Inc.
Larry Stubbs
Matt Thein
Andy Tyson

SCOTTISH STONE CRAFT

Alex Skellon
Clifford Cook
Frank Jackson
John Philips
Jason Sanders
Jesse Smokes

COASTAL READY MIX CONCRETE CO., INC.

Travis Austin
Marvin Blount
Steve Brinn
Travis Burrus
Dennis Byrd
Ronnie Clapper
Eddie Curry
Therman Dunbar
Phelpie Edmonson
Woody Fearing
Robert Flowers
Marlon Freebee
Grady Gibbs
Bobby Haywood
Glen Hodges
William Kelly
Wardell King
Willie McMurran
Stewart Moore
Wayne Morris
Jerry Owens
Billy Packer
Robert Peterson
David Quidley
Delton Simmons

Raymond Tasker
Brent Tillett
Brian Tillett
Coy Tillett, *Co-owner*
Doug Tillett
Saint Tillett, *Co-owner*
Mike Trotman
Jay Whitt
Johnny Wise

CRUM CONSTRUCTION

Jim Coleman
Lizbeth Crum
Larry Crum
Stephen Crum, *Owner*
Kelly Elliott
Charles Etheridge
Roy Good
Dennis Kailey
Ralph Lane
Dave Long
Luther Meekins
Josea Perez
Kenny Rollinson
Tammy Tinsley
Gabriel Tirado

DCF ENGINEERING, INC.

David Fischetti, *President*
John Fischetti

LAW ENGINEERING & ENVIRONMENTAL SERVICES, INC.

Jim Bailey
Randall Bailey
Brian Bellis
Candace Berry
Andy Bick
Dan Blair
Norwood Boyette
Mitzi Chaney
Victor Doritis
Charlie Greer
Thomas Hain
William Imbur
Vanessa Jamison
Robert Jenkins
Randy Knott
John Lynch
Richetta Lynch
Bob Medford
Greg Myers
Thomas Nevin

Alfredo Osuna
Pat Phelps
Cathie Sheasley
Debbie Sobeski
Shannon Sparks
Joseph Tell
John Templin
Allan Tice
Ronald Woods
Clarence Yarborough
Brett Yoho

MASONRY BUILDING CORP.
Robert Arnold
Larry Askew
Anthony Church
Brandon Davis
Robert Davis, Jr.
Ronnie Decker
Dwayne Deininger
Stephen Diaz
Archie Foreman
Phillip Grayson
Robert Hardee
Derrick Huff
Michael Lavender
Richard Lavender
Gregory Metcalfe
Glynn Parker
Bryan Roberts
Gordon Ross
James Schucker
Jeffery Spurgeon
Jangus Teger
JP Teger
Leo Walton III
Nicholas Walton

QUIBLE & ASSOCIATES
Sean Boyle
David Neff
Marilyn Seal

S. T. BARNES, INC.
Scott Barnes, Owner
Larry Barrington
James Baum
Roudolph Baum
William Bunch
Wilmer Cottingham
Randy Decker
Dwayne Duda
Allen Harris

David Jones
Franklin Melson
Kennedy Swisher
Richard Townsend
Elijah Whidbee
William Whidbee

SEABOARD SURVEYING & PLANNING, INC.
Greg Cude
Todd Grant
John Mayne
Ray Meekins
Bill Owen
Mark Perko
Carla Schoonmaker
Cawood South

WISS, JANNEY, ELSTNER ASSOCIATES, INC.
Gil Blake
Joan Crowe
Sun-Young Hong
Harry Hunderman
Steve Kelley
Rich Kristie
John Lesak
Ross Martinek
Steve Michael
Andy Osborn
Roger Pelletier
Deborah Slaton
Jerry Stockbridge
Peter Stork
Leo Zegler

CAPE HATTERAS ELECTRIC COOPERATIVE
Bill Barksdale
Tom Batchelor
Dave Conley
Donnie Farrow
Earl Fountain
Belton Gray
Michael Gray
Sandy Gray
Kerry Hooper
Gary Tolson
Howard Tolson
Lonnie Woods

WRAL-TV
Richard Adkins
Keith Baker
Terry Cantrell
Mark Copeland
John Cox
Chad Flowers
Lynn French
Joe Frieda
Gil Hollingsworth
Jay Jennings
David Renner
Ed Wilson

The railroad type crossing sign designed by Shelley Rollinson, was signed by workers and other participants in the move.

BIBLIOGRAPHY

References to consult for the early history of Cape Hatteras Lighthouse, which are readily available, include:

Dawson Carr, *The Cape Hatteras Lighthouse: Sentinel of the Shoals.* Chapel Hill: University of North Carolina Press, 2000, rev. ed.

Thomas J. Schoenbaum, *Islands, Capes, and Sounds: The North Carolina Coast.* Winston-Salem: John F. Blair, Publisher, 1982.

David Stick, *North Carolina Lighthouses.* Raleigh: North Carolina Division of Archives and History, 14th printing, 1999.

Thomas Yocum, Bruce Roberts, and Cheryl Shelton-Roberts, *Cape Hatteras, America's Lighthouse: Guardian of the Graveyard of the Atlantic.* Nashville: Cumberland House, 1999.

The best scholarly history, but one that is difficult to find, is R. Ross Holland Jr., *A History of the Cape Hatteras Light Station.* Washington, D.C.: National Park Service, 1968.

A standard reference on Outer Banks shipwrecks is David Stick, *Graveyard of the Atlantic: Shipwrecks of the North Carolina Coast.* Chapel Hill, NC: University of North Carolina Press, 1952.

SOURCE NOTES

CHAPTER I

1 Captain Lyman Jackson, *History of the 6th New Hampshire Regiment in the War for the Union*, Concord, NH: Republican Press Assoc., 1891; S. G. Griffin, *A History of the Town of Keene*, Keene, NH: Sentinel Printing Co., 1904; Hartman Bache, "Report of the Topographical Bureau, Bureau of Topographical Engineers," Nov. 14, 1861; letter, Gen. Ambrose Burnside to Lt. Col. James H. Simpson, Dec. 25, 1863, which was written in support of Simpson's promotion. Details of Simpson's career were taken from his military records, National Archives and Records Administration. After Simpson's death from pneumonia in St. Paul, Minnesota, in 1883, the Committee of Pensions listed his periods and places of service for the record.

CHAPTER 2

1 An authoritative source on lightships is provided by Willard Flint, *Lightships of the United States Government*, Washington, D.C.: U.S. Coast Guard, 1989.

2 The "text book" for dune construction on the Outer Banks was written by A. C. Stratton and James R. Hollowell, "Methods of Sand Fixation and Beach Erosion Control," July 1940. In their report, they trace the first sand fences to the first decade of the twentieth century, when two hunting clubs used fencing to restore their properties on Bodie and Pea Islands (pp. 10-11).

3 Roger W. Toll, "Report on Cape Hatteras Ocean Beach Project to the Director, National Park Service," Nov. 26, 1934; letter, A. E. Demaray, Associate Director, National Park Service (NPS), to Frank Stick, Dec. 22, 1934.

4 Letter, Stick to Demaray, Feb. 27, 1935. Note, Arno B. Cammerer to Demaray, Mar. 2, 1935.

5 Letter, Conrad C. Wirth, Assistant Director, NPS, to 3d Regional Officer, NPS, June 7, 1935. Memo, Verne E. Chatelain, Acting Assistant Director, to Cammerer, July 22, 1936.

6 Letter, Congressman Lindsay C. Warren to Harold L. Ickes, Secretary, Department of the Interior, July 16, 1935. Memo, A. P. Stauffer, Assistant Historian, NPS, to Chatelain, July 17, 1936.

7 "Dare County~Full Speed Ahead," *Coastland Times*, vol. 1, no. 5, Aug. 2, 1935.

8 Memo, Ben H. Thompson, personal assistant to Cammerer, Sept. 10, 1935.

9 Harlan D. Unrau and G. Frank Williss, "Administrative History: Expansion of the National Park Service in the 1930s," NPS report, Denver Service Center, Sept. 1983, p. 109.

10 Memo, Cammerer to Ickes, July 29, 1936; memo, Demaray to W. B. Fry, Department of Commerce, July 27, 1936; letter, Asst. Sec. of Commerce to Ickes, Oct. 20, 1936; press release, NPS, Nov. 25, 1936; letter, Wirth to E. J. Byrum, Cape Hatteras State Park, "Maintenance Cape Hatteras Lighthouse," Dec. 17, 1936.

11 Memo, Byrum to Custodian Dough, Kill Devil Hill Monument, Aug. 29, 1939.

12 Report, untitled, to Secretary, Department of the Interior, on legislation, Apr. 9, 1937; House of Representatives, Committee on Public Lands, HR7022 report, July 22, 1937.

13 Plans and Design Branch, NPS, "Final Recommendations," Nov. 8, 1937.

14 Letter, Herbert Evison, Acting Reg. Dir., ECW Reg. 1, NPS, to Cammerer, Oct. 26, 1937; memo, Earl A. Trager, Chief, Naturalist Div., NPS, to Cammerer et al., "Preliminary Report on Cape Hatteras Area," Nov. 27, 1937.

15 Letter, Thomas J. Allen, Regional Director, Reg. 1, NOS, to Chester S. Davis, *Winston-Salem Journal & Sentinel*, May 29, 1947.

16 Memo, Arthur F. Perkins, Park Planner, to Regional Director, Nov. 8, 1948.

17 Memo, Allen to Conrad L. Wirth, "Report on Meeting Regarding Cape Hatteras National Seashore Project," Aug. 1, 1950; letter, Wirth to George R. Ross, North Carolina Department of Conservation and Development, Feb. 13, 1950.

18 "Information on Request from National Park Service for Additional $200,000 Allocation to Complete Acquisition at Cape Hatteras National Seashore Recreational Area," Sept. 19, 1957.

19 NPS, "Cape Hatteras National Seashore Recreational Area Project, Some Questions and Answers," 1952, p. 9; Wirth, "A Letter to the People of the Outer Banks," Oct. 27, 1952, published in *The Coastland Times*, Oct. 31, 1952.

20 Department of the Army, Coastal Engineering Research Center, "Beach Erosion Study, U.S. Naval Facility, Cape Hatteras, Buxton, North Carolina," 1967.

21 Denver Service Center, NPS, "Environmental Assessment, Cape Hatteras Shoreline Erosion Policy Statement," Nov. 1974.

22 Dirk Frankenberg, *The Nature of the Outer Banks: Environmental Processes, Field Sites, and Development Issues, Corolla to Ocracoke*, Chapel Hill: University of North Carolina Press, 1995, p. 4.

23 Denver Service Center, NPS, "Environmental Assessment, Cape Hatteras Shoreline Erosion Policy Statement," Nov. 1974, pp. 76-122.

24 Letter, Orrin H. Pilkey to Regional Director, Southeast Region, NPS, Dec. 19, 1974.

25 Letter, Arthur W. Cooper, Assistant Secretary, North Carolina Department of Natural and Economic Resources, to James Dunning, Supt., Cape Hatteras National Seashore, Feb. 20, 1975.

26 Cape Hatteras National Seashore, NPS, "Barrier Island Environmental Management Policy, Cape Hatteras National Seashore," Mar. 1975.

27 NPS, "Status Report: Seashore Management Strategy, Cape Hatteras National Seashore, North Carolina," Oct. 1978, pp. 16-17.

28 MTMA Design Group and Department of Marine Science and Engineering, North Carolina State University, "Study Report, Cape Hatteras Lighthouse," Dec. 1980.

29 Denver Service Center, NPS, "Environmental Assessment, General Management Plan/Development Concept Plan," July 1981. The National Parks and Recreation Act of 1978 requires a general management plan for each park unit. The process for preparing such a plan is tedious: an environmental assessment, general management plan, and development concept plan is prepared, documenting existing conditions and presenting options for future actions and the consequences of those actions. During that assessment, the comments of government agencies and residents are sought. Agencies and the public are again asked to respond, this time to the draft plan. Based on the recommendations of the regional director, further environmental documentation may be called for, such as an impact statement (which can take years to prepare), and revisions to the document made. An amended environmental assessment, general management plan, and development concept plan for Cape Hatteras was completed in January 1984 and approved by the regional director in May. It can take years to prepare a general management plan. By the time the final reviews and revisions have been made, it is not unlikely that national and regional priorities have changed, as well as the leadership of the National Park Service.

30 Lee Wan & Associates, "Cost Estimate for Segmental Relocation and Reconstruction of the Historical Lighthouse at Cape Hatteras, Buxton, North Carolina," May 31, 1982; draft paper, Pilkey, David M. Bush, and William J. Neal, "Lessons from Lighthouses: Shifting Sands, Coastal Management Strategies, and the Cape Hatteras Lighthouse Controversy," Nov. 10, 1998.

31 Lorance Dix Lisle and Robert Dolan, "Coastal Erosion at Cape Hatteras: A Lighthouse in Danger," NPS Research/Resources Management Report SER-65, 1983, pp. iv, 39-43.

32 Letter, David C. Fischetti to Hugh Morton, Aug. 8, 1983.

33 North Carolina Department of Natural Resources and Community Development, "Coastal Resources Commission's Outer Banks Erosion Task Force Report," July 1984.

34 Denver Service Center, NPS, "General Management Plan, Development Concept Plan, Amended Environmental Assessment, Cape Hatteras National Seashore, North Carolina," Jan. 1984, p. 57.

35 Letter, Fischetti to Russell E. Dickenson, Director, NPS, Dec. 29, 1986; letter, David M. Bush to Representative Walter B. Jones, Feb. 18, 1987; letter, Barrett Wilson to Thomas L. Hartman, Superintendent, Cape Hatteras National Seashore, Feb. 27, 1987; letter, Save the Lighthouse Committee, to President Ronald Reagan, Mar. 5, 1987; Daniel G. Knaebe, President, Heavy-Haul International, to Jones, Mar. 11, 1987; letter, Wilson to F. Dominic Dottavio, Chief Scientist, Southeast Region, NPS, Mar. 20, 1987.

36 Memo, George W. Walter to Superintendent, Cape Canaveral National Seashore, Dec. 3, 1980; memo, Chief, Cultural Preservation, Southeast Region, NPS, to Superintendent, Cape Hatteras National Seashore, Dec. 16, 1980; letter, Col. Wayne A. Hanson, District Engineer, Corps of Engineers, to Senator Jesse Helms, Dec. 16, 1985; letter, Charles R. Thomas to Hartman, Apr. 10, 1987; William S. Price Jr., State Historic Preservation Officer, to Hartman, May 12, 1987.

37 Minutes, Board on Environmental Studies and Toxicology meeting, May 14-15, 1987; contract CX-5000-7-0040, between NPS, Department of Interior, and National Academy of Sciences, July 17, 1987.

38 Memo, Regional Director, Southeast Region, NPS, to Director, NPS, "Cape Hatteras Lighthouse," Nov. 18, 1987.

39 Committee on Options for Preserving Cape Hatteras Lighthouse, Board on Environmental Studies and Toxicology, Commission on Physical Sciences, Mathematics, and Resources, National Research Council, "Saving Cape Hatteras Lighthouse from the Sea: Options and Policy Implications," National Academy Press, Washington, D.C.: 1988, pp. 54-55, 71-72.

40 Memo, Acting Regional Director, Southeast Region, NPS, to Director, NPS, "Cape Hatteras Lighthouse," Mar. 17, 1988; memo, Superintendent, Cape Hatteras National Seashore, to Associate Regional Director, Planning and Compliance, Southeast Region, NPS, "Park's Comments Re: NAS Report, Options and Policy Implications, Cape Hatteras Lighthouse," May 25, 1988.

41 Memo, Superintendent, Cape Hatteras Group, to Regional Director, Southeast Region. "Assessment of Public Responses to Cape Hatteras Lighthouse Protection Alternatives," Sept. 20, 1989; memo, Regional Director, Southeast Region, to Director, NPS, "Decision on Cape Hatteras Lighthouse," Nov. 16, 1989.

42 Letter, Dolan to Dottavio, Oct. 19, 1992; memo, Deputy Associate Regional Director, Natural Resource Management and Science, Southeast Region, NPS, to Superintendent, Cape Hatteras National Seashore, "Location of Cape Hatteras Lighthouse," Oct. 29, 1992; "Report and Recommendations from a Committee that Reviewed the Erosion Problem at Cape Hatteras and the Risks to the Cape Hatteras Lighthouse," Dec. 1992.

43 Memo, Superintendent, Cape Hatteras Group, to Regional Director, Southeast Region, "Cape Hatteras Lighthouse Long-Term Protection," Mar. 11, 1993.

44 Letter, Amy R. Gillispie, Assistant Attorney General, Department of Justice, North Carolina, to Ries Collier, Sept. 11, 1996; memo, Superintendent, Cape Hatteras Group, to Regional Director, Southeast Region, "North Carolina Coastal Resources Commission Hearing, Cape Hatteras Lighthouse Fourth Groin," Sept. 20, 1996.

45 Ad Hoc Committee of Faculty, North Carolina State University, "Saving the Cape Hatteras Lighthouse from the Sea," Jan. 1997.

46 John E. Cornelison Jr., "Phase 1 Archeological Testing of the Cape Hatteras Lighthouse Complex Prior to Relocation," SEAC Accession 1290, Park Accession 149, Southeast Archeological Center, National Park Service, Aug. 2000; "Project Agreement, Move Cape Hatteras Lighthouse," Apr. 4, 1997.

47 Dare County Board of Supervisors, "Resolution: Protection of Cape Hatteras Lighthouse," Nov. 3, 1997.

48 News release, Cape Hatteras Group, NPS, "National Park Service Explains Its Position on the Relocation of the Cape Hatteras Lighthouse," Apr. 2, 1998; letter, Robert W. Reynolds, Superintendent, Cape Hatteras Group, to Geneva H. Perry, Chairman, Dare County Board of Commissioners, Nov. 25, 1998.

49 Joseph J. Jakubik, Project Manager, International Chimney Corporation, "Initial Proposal, Design and Construction (Design/Build) Contract to Relocate Cape Hatteras Light Station," Apr. 15, 1998.

CHAPTER 3

1 Denver Service Center, NPS, "Relocate the Cape Hatteras Light Station, Package CAHA 175, Request for Proposal," Feb. 18, 1998, p. 4.

2 Agenda, "National Park Service Value Analysis Study, Cape Hatteras Lighthouse Site Development and Restoration," Dec. 9-11, 1997.

3 Denver Service Center, NPS, "Relocate the Cape Hatteras Light Station, Package CAHA 175, Request for Proposal," Feb. 18, 1998, pp. 7-8.

4 International Chimney Corp. (ICC), "Reference Information on International Chimney Corporation," 1999.

5 ICC, "Initial Proposal, Design and Construction (Design/Build) Contract to Relocate Cape Hatteras Light Station," Apr. 15, 1998, p. 3.

6 ICC, "Initial Proposal, Design and Construction (Design/Build) Contract to Relocate Cape Hatteras Light Station," Apr. 15, 1998.

CHAPTER 4

1 Dirk Frankenberg, *The Nature of the Outer Banks: Environmental Processes, Field Sites, and Development Issues, Corolla to Ocracoke,* Chapel Hill: University of North Carolina Press, 1995, pp. 26-29.

2 ICC, "Initial Proposal, Design and Construction (Design/Build) Contract to Relocate Cape Hatteras Light Station," Apr. 15, 1998, pp. 6-7; and ICC, "Specification, Final, Relocate the Cape Hatteras Light Station, Cape Hatteras National Seashore, NC, for U.S. Department of the Interior, National Park Service, Denver Service Center," Apr. 12, 1999, pp. 2.23-1 through 2.23-3.

CHAPTER 6

1 News release, U.S. Department of Interior, NPS, Outer Banks Group, "Cape Hatteras Lighthouse Remains Straight as an Arrow," July 17, 2000.

2 e-mail, Robert E. Woody to Lin Ezell, Sept. 7, 2000.

3 Telecon, Tom Skinner and Ezell, Aug. 5, 1999.

4 Daniel C. Couch, "Islanders Share Their Lighthouse Memories," *Island Breeze,* Special Edition, summer 1999, pp. 48-53.

5 Irene Nolan, "A Triumph of the Human Mind and Spirit," *Island Breeze,* Special Edition, summer 1999, pp. 4-5.

6 Letter, Joe Jakubik to Ezell, Oct. 6, 2000.

7 Telecon, Bill Harris and Ezell, Sept. 27, 2000.

8 Interview, Dan McClarren with Ezell, Sept. 28, 2000.

9 Robert E. Woody, "Observations on the Significance of the Cape Hatteras Lighthouse Move," Sept. 7, 2000.

INDEX

Note: The photograph and graphics credit lines, appendices, bibliography, and source notes are *not* included in this index. For a listing of all project participants, see Appendix B.